DADDY'S GIRL

Daddy's Girl

THE WAITING GAME

Angelavette Williams-Hawkins

Editor/Proofreader
Terell "LeShawnspeaks" Williams
TerellWilliams1983@gmail.com

Cover by
Mr. Dale L. Stoudmire of The Stoudmire Media Group, LLC

ISBN: 979-8-21810-427-6

First Printing, 2022

PRINTED IN THE UNITED STATES OF AMERICA

I would like to dedicate this book to:

My Heavenly Father, who is my creator.

My biological mom and dad, who are no longer here on Earth,
but will forever live in my heart.

My god mother and three spiritual dads who played a crucial
role in my spiritual guidance and taught me the importance of
operating in faith, Co-Pastor Anita Spaulding, Bishop Richard
Spaulding, Bishop Stacey McQueen
and Bishop Anthony Gilyard.

My children, who are and have been such a blessing and
encouragement throughout my waiting process.

My husband, for showing up and being everything I prayed for
— making my wait worthwhile.

Contents

Prologue

How appropriate that I was asked to write the prologue for the second book from the Daddy's Girl series entitled *"Daddy's Girl: The Waiting Game"*. Firstly, I can relate to the thoughts and feelings of many of the authors in the book. While it is often assumed that women are the ones waiting for the right mate to appear, there are men who also go through a process of playing the waiting game. Rather than playing the waiting game I was playing the avoidance game and dodging the opportunity to meet a suitable mate after experiencing a toxic and stress-filled marriage. I still kept my eyes and heart open for the possibility of meeting the proverbial "Ms. Right". By divine intervention I met the visionary author of this book during my recovery from the overdose of spousal mistreatment, selfishness, disrespect and infidelity. We were both washing away the sour taste of our failed marriages and were cautiously optimistic about going down the rocky road of matrimony for a second time. Fortunately for us the road was paved with love, mutual respect, open and honest communication and other key ingredients to a recipe for a lasting relationship.

Secondly, since I've met and spent time with several of the authors I am familiar with their stories and can attest to the weight they've had to carry as they waited for that suitable mate to enter their lives.

This anthology explores the thoughts, feelings, and experiences of women who have waited for Mr. Right to show up. The game of waiting can create as much anxiety for women as a gambler who is waiting for that next card in the high stakes of a Black Jack game…. sometimes you win, sometimes you lose. Some women will eventually hit the jackpot while others will wait for the next hand to be dealt.

It's very important that women have a happy and healthy Daddy-Daughter relationship because the father serves as the first example of how a man treats a woman. How men treat their daughters, wives, mothers, and other women in their circle provides an important barometer by which women will judge and select their mates.

These stories will provide you with the confidence that there is a suitable mate waiting to meet you, but you have to be ready to drop the weight of the wait and learn to love who you are. Once you love yourself the wait will be over because the weight of expectation will be lightened enough for you to carry any load!

Derek Hawkins
Husband, Father, Brother & Son
Author of *CRACKING THE DADDY CODE: The Importance of Developing a Fulfilling Father & Son Relationship*

Angelavette Williams-Hawkins

1

Detour To The Open Door

From my observations and life interactions, most people develop an interest in dating in their late middle school or early high school years. During their primitive years, children are mostly influenced by their parents or guardians. However, if there are no healthy examples in the home to glean from, the children generally seek attention on the outside of the home, mainly from their peers. Once a child is ready to start dating they tend to become attracted to choices that are similar to examples they have seen in their past; or, they are likely to connect with a particular "type." This "type" or personal choice, is not always so personal in its formation, but more so influenced by what they have been told.

According to Genesis, the union of man and woman began with the creation of man. He was created to be head of the house. He was formed with the necessary components to procreate and build the family. He was fashioned with physical strength. He was granted the heavy burden of leading the way as a guide and protector for the woman. Unfortunately, since the beginning of time, man has struggled to operate in this call placed on them.

The Bible lets us know that a man who finds a wife finds a good thing. Men, when God sends your good thing, she is authentic, organic, and irreplaceable. It's important to understand that what looks good to the eye is not always good for the soul. So, when God sends your good thing, remain focused on her and her needs.

Imagine being that man who is the God-intended embodiment of love and respect for women. Imagine being molded into a model husband figure. Imagine being that man who is the perfect example for the seed that was gifted to you. Imagine being the man who demonstrates for his daughter how a man should properly treat them. What's imaginable can manifest into reality. Although the man has been hit with many obstacles that prohibit him from assuming these positions and functioning in his intended purpose, there is hope. The journey isn't always easy; but, the key is putting in the work to become in tune with the needs of the woman that you are assigned to.

It is safe to say that every woman desires to be loved by a man at some point in her life, whether it be her biological daddy, step daddy, grand daddy, god daddy, pastor who serves as a spiritual daddy, or perhaps a mentor who took on the role to help rear her in the direction of understanding proper love. If she is loved properly, she will function at her best form as a woman. With love comes respect. As a man, you should always be cognizant of your interactions with the women in your life. Respect should be prioritizing agenda. Respect is one of the key elements to building her self esteem.

I was blessed to have an example of the respect factor: my father. As a father, he exemplified respect and pushed me to demand nothing less than the respect that's due to me. I've always found myself to be an obedient young lady while growing up, honoring the thoughts and perspectives of my parents, especially my dad. In fact, in retrospect, I remember choosing my very first date based on my father's perspective of how a man should be. One thing my father admonished me was: "you should date an intellectually educated man." He believed that you couldn't go wrong if you partnered with a man of a certain intellect, who is apt to making informed decisions. So, when I developed interests in males, I considered their academic background and approach of prioritizing their education.

The first guy that I took seriously was someone I met in high school. A good friend of mine introduced us after he shared with her that he was highly interested in me. He was one of the most studious and artistically gifted young men in the school. Knowing that I would be intrigued, she emphatically said to me, "this guy is a straight A student." Predictably, I was engaged and wanted to know more about him.

I took it upon myself, without the consent of my dad or mom, to start dating him. I made my decision with my dad's perspective in mind; so, I just assumed all would be fine. A whole year transpired and I hadn't introduced him to my parents because the majority of our time was spent during school hours and walking home from school. We also spent time on the phone. As time progressed, we developed a seriousness towards one another. We had several discussions about breaking my virginity. After several times of me telling him "no," I finally gave in and experienced feelings of guilt, shame, disappointment, and various emotions that clouded my mind shortly after.

I couldn't believe I found myself contradicting, not only the morals that my dad and mom had instilled in me, but my own spiritual convictions as well. My emotions were haywire. The mental torment of wanting to share my act of disobedience with my parents followed me everyday. I was also angry at him for asking me several times. Perhaps it was the peer pressure that got to me. Although he was every young girl's dream and had the qualities that my dad approved of, our relationship didn't withstand the anger and disappointment I held towards both of us.

Five months later, my dad learned that I broke my virginity, not because I was brave enough to share that information with him, but because that was the moment we discovered that I was pregnant. My mom was really infuriated; and, although my dad was angry as well, he expressed mixed emotions as he found joy in the thought of the birth of his first grandchild — the anger completely dissipated upon my son entering the world.

During the 80's, it was common for society to make a young girl feel as if it was a mistake to become pregnant at an early age and out of wedlock; but, my parents were very supportive. Their supportive nature is the reason I was able to develop into the best mom I could. They never treated him like a mistake — I kept living my life. I continued with my education, without a struggle, and later entered into a successful career.

Once I overcame that hurdle, I was able to appreciate the value in it as a dating lesson that would live with me for the rest of my life. As I grew older, I became wiser. I was more comfortable with introducing guys to my dad. He would say to them, "nice to meet you for the first and last time because my daughter doesn't stay with them long." For me, long could have been two days, two weeks, or two months. At this point in my life, I had no desire to waste time with dead weight.

By that time, I didn't just have to fend for myself, I had to protect the best interest of my son. The dating game had changed. I had to be cognizant of what my dad taught me, as well as who was best to bring into my son's life. When my son was just two years old, I was happy to meet who I thought was my soul mate. He was a blessing during this pivotal point in my life. The greatest thing about meeting him was that he was handsome, smart, talented, humble, spiritually inclined, trustworthy, and someone who loved my son. I don't believe things happen by chance. God ordained our paths to cross.

In the beginning of our relationship, I established rules regarding not being pressured into sex. My goal was to meet someone who had the same long term dating goals. Another prerequisite was the priority of education and a strong bond with my son. We hit it off very well for about seven years. Our families believed that we would get married and have a long lasting relationship. Although my son's father was a part of his life, this gentleman, along with my father, served as a great role model for my son.

Though we were what most would call the perfect couple, I had to learn another lesson: people enter your life for a reason, a season, or a lifetime. This young man was a keeper. We meshed very well. I really admired the fact that my son was treated as his own. To add to this, my dad liked and accepted him. He spent many days with and around my family, as I did with his. But, sometimes in life we have to know when to let go and move on. This was my time to become aware of this. He went away to the Navy and I went to college. Unfortunately, after a few years, we grew apart. We still remained in contact, to a certain degree.

A few years went by without the need for me to take any man seriously in dating. However, I went on a few mini dates — more like hanging out; however, none of those dates developed into a meaningful relationship. At this point my son was a little older — nine years old with the ability to understand that it was time for me to start dating again and he could take part in that decision.

It was the year 1990 when my family had a family reunion in the South, where my mom and dad were originally born and raised. During the reunion my cousin advised me that an old male friend that I grew up with wanted to see me. At the time, I wasn't dating. So, I thought it wouldn't hurt to have a friendly conversation, especially since our families were very close; and, the fact that my mom babysat for his mom and dad added to my ease.

Sometimes we desire to date the perfect mate. Our desires lead us into entering into relationships, sometimes rather swiftly, without cautious considerations of the outcomes; but, even in those Russian roulette adventures, we can find valuable lessons. Your experiences in this waiting process will either make you a better person, tear at your self-esteem, or cause you to develop a guard as hard as the Jericho wall. In the event that a wall is built, you risk obscuring your view of who the ultimate Daddy has for you. This wall will cause a blockade to your heart, preventing a destiny-designed mate from entering. In my case, it helped me to realize that no man exists with perfection — they can be great in many areas but have room for growth in others. Furthermore, I came face to face with that lesson my daddy wanted me to learn: do not accept less than what you deserve. I learned to set boundaries at the door. I began to develop the practice of leading them to the exit door, if they didn't present themselves to be a match for me. Sometimes what didn't work out for you, really did work out for you.

I was determined to never settle to be with someone who didn't meet the standards of what my daddy taught me to seek. I wanted every man to treat me exactly like my dad. In my younger days, I thought of my dad as the perfect example of a man. So, the bar was set high. Setting the bar doesn't necessarily denote that you'll never slip into a bad relationship. We all become vulnerable at times. It's human nature. It does, however, demand a level of discernment to determine when it's time to free yourself from a toxic situation.

With maturity, came my increased discernment. When I finally connected with my first husband, I thought the wait was over. He was a hard worker, like my dad. He was a comedian. He knew how to make me laugh. He believed in spoiling me. He also accepted my son as his own. We became married and had a beautiful, intelligent, gifted, baby girl.

Twelve years later, I made the decision to move on and get a divorce. This was not a mistake, but another lesson learned. Each lesson made me a better woman for the man that God would have for me. After our divorce, I became a single mom of two, I became unstoppable, as I was determined to be a sufficient provider for my children. Being single was not an excuse for my children to lack their necessities and desires.

As I moved forward into the dating scene this time around, I set the bar even higher; and, although I knew what not to allow, I became more rational in my expectations. I grew wiser and more socially aware. I couldn't depend on a man to do exactly what my father did, as I was more independent and self-sufficient.

Dating was frustrating at times, until I figured out a way to take the weight of the wait off of my conscience. I no longer felt the need to change him to be a duplicate of my dad. I anticipated that the right one would come ready to grow with me. I also grasped the understanding that men and women speak different love languages. Men process things differently than women. Communication is a key factor in dating; and, the lack thereof can consequently be one of the biggest failures in relationships. Past trauma and/or the lack of proper male figures in their lives can hinder their ability to communicate effectively.

The manner in which a man was raised determines how well he communicates with a woman. Knowing this, instead of becoming flustered and annoyed, we should tap into our nature of being sympathetic and compassionate. Become the solution to his problem. As women, we are called to be man's helpmate. Your tone and approach should come from a place of support and sympathy. Moreover, it's crucial to invest the proper time needed to learn his love language. This will yield greater results in his communication with you. Conversely, men should invest time in building the respect factor. With love, comes respect. If she is loved right, she will function at her best form as a woman. In my case, I learned this lesson and successfully balanced it with my position as a Daddy's Girl.

Daddy Girl Effect (On Me):

#1 **I Learned Independence**. Being raised as daddy's girl encompasses more than just being "spoiled." I am independent enough to have my own, but wise enough to understand that men have a desire to feel needed to a certain extent. I always had my own. So, whenever I did meet a man, I wasn't in a position to solely depend on him. Rather, I was prepared to enhance and add to his accomplishments and visa versa.

#2 **I Was Raised To Have A High Level Of Standards.** Long before Steve Harvey came out with his book "Act Like a Lady, Think Like a Man," my dad had instilled that life approach in me. Thus, when that man came into my life, I knew how a lady should be treated. I knew and understood what chivalry was, although I had no problem opening the door for myself, buying roses for myself, or taking myself to dinner. When that special man came into my life, I gave him the opportunity to mesmerize me as a knight in shining armor. When a man meets and supersedes his duties in his chivalrous nature, he should be provided with security in knowing that he is appreciated.

#3 **I Was Taught To Give And Command Respect.** As I grew into my womanhood, I understood that respect is crucial. As I evolved into a Proverbs 31 woman, I comprehended the assignment even more, knowing that respect is reciprocal. If two people can't respect one another in all aspects of life while in a relationship, it's time to exit. Staying in a relationship that's not conducive to your self worth or growth can become very toxic.

Sometimes she never recovers her self respect; other times it takes so much longer to do so because of the walls of protection she's built to save herself from further damage to her heart.

Paying attention and learning the love language of your partner early in the dating process plays a major role in the wait. Learning their likes vs dislikes and comfort vs discomfort factors is key to capturing their undivided attention. I call it "cracking the code to matters of his heart." Once you've cracked the code to his heart, then more weight in the waiting game has been lifted. In many instances, this will open the door for the man to move forward in the process with you. There are gains to this waiting game.

Now that you have cracked the code and are closer to your prized possession, there are more steps to this game. While you are waiting for him to put that diamond ring on your finger, don't give up so easily by letting him test your sacred diamond. When he finally asks the question and puts a ring on it, continue to make the wait worth it. A ring doesn't mean he's earned the goods. It's your body and mind. You are the decision maker, the deal breaker. Don't allow the pressure from the diamond to crush your decision. If it's your ultimate desire to get married then continue to stand on your beliefs.

After having many conversations with women I learned that not all have the same value and beliefs in dating and relationships. Some shared stories of becoming engaged and waiting as long as ten to fifteen plus years to get married — some even longer. To each its own. For me, it's more than just a ring on the finger. I was raised to understand that marriage is a sacred covenant between two. The Bible explains that marriage between a man and woman is honorable in the sight of God.

A man and woman coming together with the same purpose makes dating so much more valuable. A man that was raised with morals and values will become a man who respects and appreciates her making him wait. It's just like respecting his time while she waits for him to go from dating, to engaged, to married. Women, your time is valuable. It is your responsibility to pay attention to signs. Be aware of behaviors that are esteem destroyers. If you discover that he operates with an excessively controlling nature, be courageous enough to exit.

As women we were created from the man's rib, built as a multi-tasking engine. We are equipped to weather the storm in the waiting process. We give birth to him, we nurture him, we feed him, we train him to become a man, we marry him, we give birth to his children. Without women, reproduction is impossible. The presence of women leads men to their understanding of intimacy. Women play a major role in helping men operate in chivalry and with affection. Women, we are the queens of their castle.

Once you know, understand, and believe how valuable you are to a man that's when the game changes. You are no longer the victim but the victor. You will now know the difference between a grown man and a boy. You will begin to treat them accordingly. A boy in a man's body likes toys they can play around with. They will hold you hostage in a relationship as long as you stay and accept the games he's playing. A man, on the other hand, values a strong, confident, classy woman who walks with dignity. He recognizes initially who he can bring home to his mother.

When you challenge him to wait, you become his heavyweight — heavy on understanding your assignment, heavy on staying strong in your assignment, and heavy on becoming successful in your assignment.

He then crowns you, treating you like a queen — like the ones he observed in his past.

Queens don't tear men down; neither do they tear down or contribute to tearing down another woman's relationship/marriage. Queens are strong, classy, confident women. They don't covet what belongs to other women. She waits her turn and understands that when the right one comes along he's not just merely another man to her. He's GOD sent; and, she has earned all rights to becoming his heavyweight, his Proverbs 31 woman, his wife, his boo, and his rib — the neck that turns his head.

I would never say that sometimes the scenic route of a trip isn't annoying at times. On the flip side, I can't deny the impact of engaging with the lessons to be learned from details on that road. The scenic route takes longer, of course, but there's a level of appreciation that I've found in riding the wave and enjoying the detour.

I am so grateful for all the twists and turns that finally connected me with my husband, soul mate, Boaz, and best friend. He is not just everything that I prayed for, desired, and wrote the vision for, but he is also a daddy's dream mate for his daughter. He stepped on the scene of my life and humbly allowed God to continue to mold him. God's timing was perfect.

Although the waiting game may leave you feeling frustrated, worthless, unappreciated, exhausted, distressed, and in despair, trust the process. The process is what prepares you for the mate that God has for you. It strengthens. It helps develop you into the woman a man needs. No man or woman is perfect. If we, both parties, honor the main ingredients, respect, love, and commitment, coming together will be worthwhile. You may have to experience a detour, but if you ride the process out, you will meet your mate at the open door.

I would like to leave you with three sustaining points that helped me during my waiting process:

- Write your vision and make it clear.
- Activate your faith and trust the process.
- Know your worth and accept nothing less.

Three points of wisdom for men who are reading this:

- Seek God when choosing your mate. Allow your eyes to mirror a Godly view.
- Present yourself as a provider, protector, and pilot, helping your mate navigate through the turmoil of life. Add to her, instead of subtracting from her. Avoid making her feel as if she is a burden to you.
- Keep your eyes on your prize: your wife.

Theresa Billingsley

2

The Weight of the Wait

It was one of the most painful experiences of my life. It was like death. I felt so uncertain about the future. I was smacked in the face with one of the biggest decisions I would ever have to make in my life. I can't adequately put into words how agonizing this moment was for me, the fear of losing my children and wanting to protect them from the pain, not wanting to hurt the other party involved, the fear of how I would pay bills with no child support or alimony, the fear of who would want me after being divorced. These thoughts plagued my mind.

The moral of the story is, I was now thrust into the waiting game, and my question was, "How long would it take to heal?" I further pondered on more questions: "How long will it take for me to find myself again after suppressing so much for so long?" and "How long will it take before I am ready to date again, along with many other tormenting thoughts?" It became an emotional weight, but one thing that became apparent to me is that there is life after divorce. I had to come to the realization that I am worth the wait it takes to heal and the wait it takes to be found by my God ordained mate. If you read my chapter in, "Daddy's Girl: The Ultimate Covering", you will understand why my willingness to wait was a huge victory for me.

Disclaimer: To all of the men reading this, I love you tremendously; and, I am in no way bashing the male species. Please hear my heart! I am simply sharing my experience and wisdom on how to beware of significant signs and actions. Actually, my sincere desire is for men to benefit from the principles and concepts infused in this chapter, while offering insight on the manipulation and mind games that some, not all, women selfishly play. You may have dealt with some women who were manipulative and needy — some may have even played on your desire to be their knight in shining armor. In any event, those assigned to my voice will benefit in some way from this labor of love I have written.

What is the waiting game?

According to Merriam-Webster, the **WAITING GAME** is a strategy in which one or more participants withhold actions temporarily in the hope of having a favorable opportunity for more effective action later.

Furthermore, according to Idiom's Dictionary, the **WAITING GAME** is a situation in which one postpones or delays a decision or course of action in order to discover the opponent's next move.

Gaining Weight During the Wait

There is more than one type of weight, healthy and unhealthy. You can have the weight of God's Glory or the weight of regrets, lusts, and selfish desires on your shoulders while you wait. I prefer the weight of God's Glory. His glory has many manifestations; but, in this instance, the aspect of His glory reflects the acts and character of Christ during His earthly days, according to Vine's Expository Dictionary of Old & New Testament Words.

"And the Word was made flesh, and dwelt among us, (and we beheld his glory, the glory as of the only begotten of the Father,) full of grace and truth." (KJV John 1:14).

One day while I was praying, God revealed to me that I am a word from heaven made flesh, manifested in the earth. I profess to you that this revelation applies to you as well. When God spoke life over you from Heaven through your mother's womb, He also spoke into your destiny. To that end, you have an assignment to seek Him to unpack what is included in your destiny package. Upon doing so, you find fulfillment, avoiding carrying the weight of feeling incomplete due to being without a mate. You will have an assurance that you are complete in Him, and you won't feel the need to aimlessly search for someone to bring you happiness.

You will carry the weight of His glory, fulfilling your destiny, and not being derailed by your unmet expectations. Your wait won't be an unhealthy weight. Not to say that you're exempt from encountering challenges or uncomfortable moments, but His word assures us that the affliction is light and only for a moment not a lifetime. **"For our light affliction, which is but for a moment, worketh for us a more exceeding and eternal weight of glory. " (2 Corinthians 4:17 KJV).**

It is always "our choice" to use our free will to agree with God or to go against God's will for our lives. It's NEVER God's fault.

That is the risk God took (for lack of a better word, because, essentially, there is no such thing as God taking a risk). He created us with a will to either obey Him and love Him freely or oppose, avoid, and disobey Him. Operating against God's will for our lives will cause weight that is exasperating and tiresome. God's Word admonishes us that the way of a transgressor is hard.

"Wherefore seeing we also are compassed about with so great a cloud of witnesses, let us lay aside every Weight and the Sin which doth so easily beset us, and let us run with patience the race that is set before us." (**Hebrews 12:1 KJV**).

Notice the Word of God encourages us to lay aside every weight and the sin which doth so easily beset us; this admonishment is not intended to send the message that you lay down and give up while you wait. Don't lay down and indulge in frivolous sexual immorality. Don't give up on what you are believing God for. Don't surrender to fear or mediocrity. There's a more productive way to approach this — surrender wholeheartedly to the plan and will of God.

Have you ever realized the devil always uses God's principles, perverting them, to denounce the impact of God's Word in the lives of His people? The devil is counteractive to the Word of God; but, his power only reigns if we allow it.

God desires for us to lay aside every weight and sin, while the devil's duty is to entice us to lay aside our God ordained destinies. His job is to steal, kill, and destroy you, along with your destiny and inheritance; and, although his cunning tactics may present pleasure, it doesn't compare to what Jesus/Yeshua has prepared for you.

Don't fear the tactics of the devil. Did you know that YOU are joint heirs with Jesus? That is why the devil fights you so much. He wants to detain you, putting up a smoke screen that camouflages God's will for your life. Let's not give the devil a 2-for-1 deal. If Jesus loses part of his inheritance, by losing you, you will in turn lose the inheritance He has for you. Don't faint during the wait.

Lose The Weight of The Wait

Instead of constantly complaining and harboring negativity about your situation, which further delays your blessings, consider my notion. You can lose the traumatic mental weight of the wait through the application of God's Word. Fill yourself with the Word of God, so it can saturate your soul. This allows you to speak the life that God freely grants us instead of just merely uttering a grocery list of complaints. Out of the abundance of the heart the mouth speaks (**Matthew 12:34-36**); therefore, it is important to change what happens in your heart as it controls your thoughts and actions. This reference to the heart doesn't relate to the organ that pumps blood in your chest. It speaks to the seat of the thoughts, affections, emotions, desires, appetites, passions, purposes, endeavors of your will and character. So, if you are full of evil and negativity, that is what will radiate from you. In that event, a reprogramming of your heart with the Word of God is conducive for growth.

The Word of God is spirit, and it is life (**John 6:63**). The Word of God is alive (**Hebrews 4:12** AMPC). Why is the Word alive? Because the Word of God is Jesus. He is the Word made flesh (**John 1:1**). So, when we speak and obey the Word of God, Jesus is directly on the scene advocating for and cosigning His Word. Here are a few scriptures to use to encourage yourself during your wait. Whatever you are waiting for, wait with expectancy; and, while you are waiting declare the Word of God every day, boldly, without doubting. Doubting is counterproductive. You can also use the appropriate scriptures in the Holy Bible to fit your situation. There are scriptures to address every area of your life. A few of my trusted scriptures are:

"Casting all your cares upon Him, for He careth for you." **(1 Peter 5:7).**

"Trust in the Lord with all your heart, and do not lean on your own understanding. In all your ways acknowledge Him, and He will make straight your paths." **(Proverbs 3:5-6).**

"Wait on the Lord. Be of good courage and He will strengthen your heart. Wait on the LORD!" **(Psalms 27:14).**

"But those who trust *(while you wait)* in the LORD will find new strength. They will soar high on wings like eagles. They will run and not grow weary. They will walk and not faint." **(NLT Isaiah 40:31).**

In order to lose the weight of the wait you must be intentional about planting the Word of God in the garden of your heart or you can easily get weeds growing by default. Use the Word of God to protect your heart from bitterness, doubt, fear, hopelessness, self-sabotage, unbelief and unforgiveness, etc... Use the Word of God to examine your heart.

Shifting your concept of time is crucial to losing the weight of the wait. Instead of being weighed down by antagonizing thoughts of your biological clock ticking, reset your focus on the purpose for its ticking — the end goal. Time is a gift given to us to fulfill our God given purpose and destiny. If you are exerting too much energy on everything else other than fulfilling your God given destiny, you are wasting precious time. God's intent for us, as virtuous women, is not to be chasers of men. Being intentional with your time and who you spend it with is crucial. I remember my son telling me to beware of who I allow in my space because some only come to be leeches.

Have you ever wasted time by aggressively pursuing a man, just to realize that he was the wrong one? In the event that this happens, just acknowledge that you were wrong, and don't attempt to justify your actions and stay in a toxic, dysfunctional situation because of pride.

Ponder on what attracted you to someone you weren't meant to spend your life with. Search your soul to discover the root of your tainted decision making process. Consider this: reasons may be your failure to consult with God or lack of confidence in hearing His voice. The truth is, you don't always attract what you want, oftentimes you attract who you are. Simply put, if you are broken, you attract brokenness; and, brokenness blinds you. Essentially, you can't see clearly through a broken mirror; thus, it is not safe to trust your vision in that broken state.

Beware of the devil's deceit. Sometimes he perverts the relationship between you and someone God intended you to win into His Kingdom, leading both parties into an unproductive state with God. Furthermore, if you fail to diligently seek God and His will, you could be blind sighted, and end up sleeping with your assignment. If you find yourself in this position, use it as a learning tool, then take the time to properly heal from your soul wounds, so that demonic attraction will no longer prevail.

In that event, it's safe to say that the devil tried you and found a landing strip. Now deal with it to prevent repetition. It is necessary to have accountability partners that are governed by the Word of God, whose vision is not blurred by deception and wantonness. However, some people are stubborn. If you are the type of person which operates in the mentality of "it's all about me, myself, and I", which I call the demonic trinity, you're actually partnering with the spirits of fear, idolatry, pride, selfishness and self-preservation. There's a remedy. Confess it to God and repent (turn away from it, never to return). Make a conscious decision to lock into what God has ordained for your life. You have to be conscious of who and what you allow your spirit to partner with — you become one with who you partner with and what you partner with impacts your entire life, whether it is physically or spiritually.

What Is A Yoke?

A yoke: a wooden bar placed over the neck of a *pair* of animals so they can pull *together* — what *unites* (*joins*) two people to move (work) *together as one*, whether moving together as one for good or evil. However, you can't operate in good while the other operates in evil. Eventually, the evil will overpower the efforts of the party operating in good.

When you take Jesus' yoke upon you and learn of Him, His yoke is easy. As you learn your identity and purpose through Him, you will take on His nature, character, and authority. Conversely, if you take on the yoke of your or another's lusts or selfish desires, you take on a heavy burden of stress.

We are not animals; so, for us, a yoke can be symbolic of an agreement or partnership of entanglement. And Jesus knew that. That's why He admonished us to take His yoke upon us and learn of Him for His yoke is easy and burden is light; the devil, the enemy of our souls hates us. Furthermore, he doesn't have the ability to create anything, so he just uses what God created, steals it, and perverts it from its original intent. The enemy's yoke is always oppressive and leads to stealing, killing, and destruction of our souls and natural man. (John 10:10). Be very cognizant of who and what you come into agreement with.

Most women are naturally nurturers; and, because we are helpers by nature we like to feel needed. This opens the door for vulnerability — easy access to becoming yoked with someone who can take advantage of us. It's easy to be deceived into thinking we are being valued because we take pride in the ability to be a providing nurturer, when, in actuality, we are being used and taken advantage of, all while being totally clueless because of our pure motives.

Yet, pride can be a hidden unintentional motivation that the devil subtly creeps in and uses to ensnare many. Jesus' yoke is easy, and with it, you can find rest. Ask yourself "why" — why keep choosing what brings toxic cycles, which causes you to get set back, waste more time and cause more wounds. Why not wait? Why not endure?

Two Can Play That "Waiting" Game

Some men are prone to playing games. If a man is trying to wait you out, breaking you down to use you as a sex toy, you should strive to wait him out. There is no need to give the impression that you're anxious. God's desire is for us to counteract our anxiety with prayer. The Bible admonishes that with prayer and supplication, we can make our requests known unto God.

Sex can easily cloud your judgment; and, although sex is very tempting, it is not impossible to avoid. God will keep give you the strength to endure sexual temptations if you allow His spirit to dwell in and direct you.

Your desire to please God can outweigh your sexual desire. If you make a conscious decision to abstain from sexual sin, you'll have the ability to observe what type of man he is — if he has discipline and self-control or if he only wants you for sex. Don't allow sex to blur the lines. If he decides to leave due to your stance, let him leave. Treat him as if he's a pimple that you don't want to reappear.

If you have preexisting rejection issues, you're prone to feeling like you were rejected. In this instance, if you chase him, he'll have the upper hand. Get healed to avoid the opportunity of your soul wounds being used against you. You are worth the wait!

Waiting Is Inevitable

What do you do after you cast your cares? Simple... You wait! But don't wait and be stagnant. Furthermore, you shouldn't wallow in a pool of complaints while you wait either. Think about it. What is the job of a restaurant waiter? They serve, take orders, and meet the requests of the ones they're assigned to wait on. Likewise, as you obtain orders from our Creator, it is to your benefit to serve Him daily, which will lead you to an open door of fulfillment. Serve Him — 5-Star waitress style.

Another example of effective serving is a Lady-in-Waiting. A lady-in-waiting is a lady of a Queen's or a Princess's household appointed to wait on her — they are personal assistants to the Queen. For example, Queen Elizabeth of York, the wife of King Henry VII, had an astounding 36 ladies-in-waiting. The third wife of England's King Henry VIII, Jane Seymour, served as lady-in-waiting to his first two wives before becoming Queen herself.

Now granted, you're probably not assigned to serve the Queen of England. However, you do have the capacity to serve somewhere and someone that God assigns you to: a widow, an orphan, a women's shelter, etc. Now, let's flip the scenario. Instead of ladies-in-waiting serving a queen or princess, we serve our Heavenly Father and Jesus Christ/Yeshua, similar to a lady-in-waiting who assists the Queen by running errands, delivering messages, organizing correspondence, and accompanying her on royal tours and visits. As His Ambassadors, we can operate in the same capacity for Jesus/Yeshua.

You may not literally be a WAITress, nor a lady-in-waiting, but the concept of serving does not alter. We are servants of the Most High, God. If we delight in Him and serve as He leads, we will serve our way into a life that is complete. "Giving you the desires of your heart" does not mean He will give you the lust that your heart desires, rather He will shift your desires. When you desire what HE wants for you, you'll find peace.

He truly does want the best for us. There is no good thing that He withholds from us when we're in proper spiritual alignment. The problem arises when we do things OUR way and not HIS, then we blame Him when things go wrong.

We must always be apt to WAIT in God's presence — putting necessary time in to hear His voice clearly. Some people don't bear the confidence that they WILL hear His voice. Some don't know His voice; but, the closer you walk with Him, He will teach you how to recognize His voice. You will definitely understand that **YOU ARE WORTH THE WAIT!**

"But those who wait on the LORD Shall renew their strength. They will mount up with wings like eagles. They shall run and not be weary. They shall walk and not faint." (**NKJV Isaiah 40:31).**

Wantonness, discontentment, and frustration will prolong the wait and cause you to choose unwisely. As the saying goes, never go food shopping when you are hungry. Ask me how I know, haha!

Who knew Waiting was a Game?

I had to learn quickly that you are a contestant in the game whether you want to be or not, whether you recognize or acknowledge it or not. Play the game or get played — games have no age limits, although, I wish there were.

I am going to continue to be vulnerable and transparent in efforts to help someone else learn from my being deceived. Sin is aggressively deceptive; therefore, it's best to avoid it and not get entangled, by thinking you are smarter than the cunning nature of the enemy. We are to flee fornication and lust, not go into it by testing the waters to see if we're strong enough to fight against it. Some battles are better left alone because curiosity can lead you into battles you are not prepared for.

Hebrews 3:13 Amplified Translation states:

"But continually encourage one another every day, as long as it is called "Today" [and there is an opportunity], so that none of you will be hardened [into settled rebellion] by the deceitfulness of sin [its cleverness, delusive glamour, and sophistication].

I find it amazing that we tend to make hasty decisions, without consulting or acknowledging God. It's common to selfishly want what we want, then get body slammed by the devil and blame God, instead of taking accountability for our negligence. Why do we like to shift the blame to God instead of the devil or our own lust or disobedience?

The Word of God admonishes us to FLEE sexual immorality, not fight it or stay in it, trying to show how you can outsmart it — it says "FLEE." Do not be too consumed with the idea of your "image" being damaged by appearing to be soft or weak. FLEE for your life!"

The Amplified Bible says:

"**Run away** from sexual immorality **[in any form, whether thought or behavior, whether visual or written]**. Every *other* sin that a man commits is outside the body, but the one who is sexually immoral sins against his own body. (1 Corinth 6:18).

Sadly, I have many stories of how I allowed my ungodly, selfish desires to lead me straight into the traps of the devil. He knew how to bait and seduce me; meanwhile, I succumbed to it. Ironically, when you get trapped once, we tend to say that we won't let it happen again, but, sometimes, it does, because you refuse to acknowledge the void and wantonness that keeps you in bondage.

Let me share one of my encounters. This is rather embarrassing — but, oh well, here it goes. This is the condensed, abbreviated version. If you want all the details, feel free to contact me directly. I was minding my own business, so I thought, and little did I know, someone who I interacted with on social media had an interest in me. He watched me from afar for a year or so. Eventually, he messaged me to place an order for a product that I sold. I didn't think anything of it initially. All of a sudden, he suggested that I give him a call, pretending our conversation would be about the products. Prior to this, I received several orders from other men for my products, whether desserts or health and wellness products, who used that opportunity as an inroad to get close to me and eventually ask me out on a date, which manifested into horror stories. Therefore, when he asked me to call him, I immediately shifted into defense mode. My internal security alarm started going off — my internal rabid pit bull alerted me. I call it that, but in hindsight, I believe it was God's signal that I ignored, saying, "Intruder alert! Beware! Danger!" Of course, my response to his message revealed my obvious trust issues.

Therefore, in ignorance, I was unaware that I gave him an advantage because he knew how to calculate his responses to keep my internal alarms from beeping and going haywire. His tactics allowed him to feed my rabid pit bulls, preventing them from being on guard, all while he appeared to me as a knight in shining armor who came to heal the damsel that needed emotional healing. Yes, I indeed needed healing, but not for the purpose of being used by someone who formed a false allegiance.

The shenanigans began:

He said all the right things, convincing me to let down my guards. He spat all the lyrical enticements women like hearing — playing on the woman's love language of sweet whispers. Men are visual and women are audial! He sent me flowers, and even money. He always listened attentively, with empathy. He even prayed with me. After about 3 months, I released one layer of my walls down. We talked every day, several hours per day. He was an entrepreneur; therefore, he was afforded the liberty to communicate with me without many time constraints. I thought I had my guard up during conversation, because I realized the more I talked to someone, the more they would seep into my soul and I would start to crave their time and attention.

Allow me to be transparent, in order to continue painting this picture. I pray my story helps someone.

His voice was so sexy; and, he had a body to match. I like to take care of this temple that God entrusted me with by exercising regularly and maintaining proper nutrition. So, we had that in common. I literally had a list and he met one of my requirements on my list. Needless to say, since then I have destroyed my list. Yes, I still have standards and certain deal breakers, but my list clearly caused me to be blindsided and clouded my judgment, allowing myself to be deceived.

I thought he was the answer to my prayers, but my prayers were based upon my own lusts and selfish desires, nothing based on what I could give, but only on what I would receive. These things are temporal and have nothing to do with fulfilling God's assignment for your life. Nonetheless, I thought, during that time, that my list had a good balance of things that would meet my spiritual and natural desires.

My list included: integrity, sense of humor, no small children, willingness to attend church with me, spiritual depth vs just being a church-goer, genuine love for my children, physical fitness, healthy eating habits, financial stability, sexually compatibility, a love for traveling, no baby momma drama, no desire to have more children, excellent communication skills, maturity (not being a petty tit for tat type person), and sharp intellect.

Furthermore, I have numbers that I always see: 444, 111, or 1110. I conducted research to interpret the biblical meaning of these numbers.

Guess what? When I added the numbers together to his address, it equaled 1110; therefore, I perceived it as another sign from God.

Oh wait, I can't forget this prerequisite: I wanted to be with someone who had a desire to become married within a reasonable time. I do not believe in dating for an immensely long period of time or being used as a sex toy. On and on my list went. I thought my list was thorough; and, he seemed to match every detail. He lived out of my state; therefore, I would've had to relocate; but, I desired my sons to come also, although all of them were over 20 years of age. He, in an attempt to make things work out, was willing to employ my sons to work for his business and move them in with us until they got on their feet. I thought to myself, "Oh my goodness, this is it." He had a beautiful home and 2 spare rooms, which seemed like a perfect match. However, I was oblivious to why he had 2 spare bedrooms.

Back to that in a moment:

He talked about marrying me within 5 months of dating. Instead of that being a red flag to me, I took it as a sign that he knew what he wanted. I have heard many love stories of how a man knows what he wants, avoiding the hassle of a long decision making process. Some stories I heard of how they met and married within 3 months and are still married to this day.

I was so ready to relocate that I took him to meet my mother. Fortunately, he didn't pass the interview with her. With a wise motherly tone, she warned me, "He is not the one for you, but I'll support whatever you decide." I should have dropped him then, but no, I had to keep testing the waters.

Have you ever ignored your own internal security alarm? Always have someone you love and respect give their opinion, so they can see blind spots that you fail to see. Never be afraid to let your decisions be tested by another. If you have to keep things hidden, that is a sign that you are being rebellious. When you hide things, you tend to have an inner gut feeling that something is wrong and others won't agree.

All of my sons are protective of me — they are my bodyguards. I asked one of my sons to go meet the prospective person before I met him in person. He put on his best behavior, of course, to impress my son. My other two sons refused to meet him. I believe they were disappointed that I lowered my standards to move and marry someone so quickly that I met via social media. (No offense to those who have found love through social media; I have just not had any success with that.)

I started preparing to move despite all of the signs and objections from my family. I started downsizing, throwing away clothes, shoes, and boots. My youngest son said, "That dude got your mind fried." I can laugh about it now, but it certainly wasn't funny then. I think I was literally under a spell. (That's what happens when you allow lust to yoke you; you open the doors of your soul, giving the devil access by default, as lust is his spirit. You are in his playing field outside of the safe boundaries of God's protective word.)

I dealt with demonic lust in the form of a love spell. My son further explained, "That's why I didn't want to meet him, nor talk to him." My sons were so upset, they created group texts to vent about their frustrations with me. I didn't find that out until after the fact. (Hilarious! I absolutely love my sons.)

One evening, while spending time with him at his home, the doorbell rang. Guess who it was? Not FedEx, UPS, or a flower delivery — NO! You guessed it, it was his ex-girlfriend. (Lord, have mercy! Where is the emoji with the palm of your hand smacking your forehead?) Prior to me coming to visit him, I specifically asked if he was with anyone. He replied, "No!" I then asked him how long it had been since he was in his last relationship. I know how it is with a person you've recently broken up with. They can come right back into your life, and at the drop of a dime, kiss you, make up with you, and then dump the new victim like they never knew them.

I also asked him, "Although you say you aren't with anyone, is there anyone who thinks you are their man?" He replied again, "No!" Liar, liar pants on fire. Sadly, I later discovered that she knew I was there because she still had access to an app on her phone to see the vehicles in his driveway; and, seeing my New Jersey license plates sparked her ferocity. Well, surprise, surprise!

So, she continued to rave about that being "her house." Hence, he had two spare bedrooms to accommodate the 2 children from her previous marriage. I let him handle her because I didn't go visit him for me to end up in jail. The only time I go to jail is to visit others or do prison ministry, share the love of Jesus Christ/Yeshua, and leave THE SAME DAY. Her anger grew and she began physically attacking him, trying to push past him, yelling for him to let her get her other belongings, making a major scene in such a beautiful, quiet community. I kept thinking to myself, "Mind your business, stay calm. As long as she does not come in your face and touch you, stay out of it." When she left, he and I had it out. I was extremely infuriated. I let him know the trust was surely broken, along with our relationship. I was happy and doing fine by myself without any drama.

In an attempt to defend himself, he pathetically replied, "I can't help what another person does." He insisted that they aren't a couple anymore and that she doesn't know how to move on. I understood that to a degree, but it still didn't sit well with me. I cried profusely from the devastation and the fact that I allowed myself to get into this situation. I let it slide, trying to give him the benefit of the doubt. Days passed and he left his cell phone in the car while we were out. As he stepped out of the car, the phone rang and I noticed her name on the screen. When he returned to the car, I advised him that she called. He brushed it off. I demanded, "Call her back in front of me!" He stated that he didn't want to feed into any negativity, so he wanted to ignore her. That was unacceptable to me; my woman's intuition led me to believe that there was something more to that call.

"Call her now or I am leaving and going back home." It took a long time for him to actually comply. I didn't want to ruin the outing we were on, so I continued to have a good time and didn't mention it again until we got back to the house. After a huge squabble, he finally agreed to call her. I said to him, "When you call her, put it on speaker and don't let her know I am listening." I wanted to hear an unscripted response, which would reveal what I needed to know. I figured if she would've said something like, "I missed your call and I was calling you back", or something along the lines of them still being in a relationship, I would, at least, have clarity.

He did the complete opposite. He led the conversation by saying, "Hi, Theresa wanted me to call you and see why you called me." *(You have got to be kidding me.)* She replied, explaining to me that she returned his call, that he always calls to check on her, and that she picked the house he lives in. I decided to listen attentively. She continued with, "That nightstand in the bedroom is mine. I moved out 3 months ago because he put his hands on me and we have a court date coming soon." When I questioned him about what had occurred, he responded that he didn't want to talk about it, asking how long I was going to dwell on it.

He brushed me off, which made the situation worse. I knew it was coming to an end. However, he tried to win my trust, so he gave me access to his camera to see who travels in and out of his house. He gave me the password to his cell phone. He even gave me a key to his home. I still didn't find peace; but, he tried to use reverse psychology to express that after all he did to build my trust in him, I was still insecure. Women's intuition never lies. I returned the expensive gifts he purchased for me along with his keys and eventually deleted the app off my phone, so I wouldn't receive the alerts anymore. Although I ignored many warnings prior to that, I would've been a certified fool to remain with him after having evidence of his infidelity continually smack me in the face.

The moral to the story is: I should have waited, instead of being anxious. The word of God admonishes us to be anxious for nothing. However, I allowed my lack of patience to conquer me, only to be disappointed and immensely exploited in the end. I was bamboozled by an impostor, a counterfeit answer to my prayer — so close externally, but, internally, there was a lot missing. Integrity was missing, consideration was missing, and humility was missing. In a nutshell, the character of God/Yeshua was missing; but, all of the external components I wanted were there. The external doesn't satisfy. Character can't be counterfeited. The impostor will always manifest, because who you are innately won't hide for long.

Opposites Attract: It Can Be a Demonic Trap To Distract

The saying opposites attract seems to be the measuring stick to choosing a partner at times. I beg to differ. Opposites can, at times, distract and derail you from your purpose. You must always stay on guard to prevent the negative impacts of being derailed, as it can drain you, if you don't have the grace to deal with it. We shouldn't invest our all into situations before we assess the cost. Slow down, use discernment. Don't ignore the signs!

Is it wise to continue riding on a highway with a sign that warns you an exit is closed due to the bridge being out of commission? Would you be shocked if you drove around all the blockades and fell off the bridge?

Ignorance is not bliss, even if you ignored the sign, didn't see the sign, or misunderstood the sign. It does not change the message of the sign.

Here are a few things to consider as an example of opposites that may be frustrating:

- If he is lazy, while you are ambitious and driven, you will be highly frustrated.
- If he is a slob and you are neat, you will experience conflict.
- If you pay bills before time or on-time and he lacks money management skills, you will be stressed and annoyed.
- If your spiritual beliefs are unaligned, you will have a ginormous problem.
- If you like to travel and he doesn't, you will have an issue to address.
- If you like to cook and he only wants to eat fast food, you will have challenges dealing with his health issues.
- If you are into health and wellness, and he's not health conscious, that's a problem.
- If you have good hygiene and he doesn't, you will not desire him intimately.
- If you like to work out and stay fit and he is undisciplined, you will be unhappy.
- If he doesn't support your dreams and goals, he may end up becoming jealous of your accomplishments.

How Long is Too Long to Wait?

There's no golden rule. It is contingent upon how much time you are willing to wait. It depends on your tolerance level for being derailed from your purpose. If you truly want to be connected with your God-ordained mate, you will wait! Waiting is better than being entangled with disappointment. Worship while you wait. God will sustain you while you wait.

The time that you regret wasting can be redeemed; and, it will be like you never missed a beat. If you've fallen out of line, God can accelerate time and put you where you would have been had you never messed up or disobeyed Him. All things are possible if you believe!

The Waiting Game (3 healing steps)

1. Seek God's will for your life & don't settle for anything/anyone less — make good use of your gift of time by SEEKING God. You will have to give an account for what you have done with your life; therefore, it would behoove you to follow the blueprint that Jesus has laid out for you. He desires the absolute best for you.

2. Make fellowship and time with God your highest priority, ask Him to reveal your unique assignments and gifts. He has given you an assignment to fulfill on Earth. Knowing your purpose would help you to avoid settling.

3. Break demonic covenants and agreements you made, knowingly and unknowingly. Identify open doors you left open to evil and close the doors. Ask God for forgiveness and cleansing. Address the root of what causes demonic cycles. Don't forget the lessons you've learned in past relationships, or you are bound to repeat it — Learn and Live! Seek professional counseling if needed. As a Certified Dietary Supplements Advisor, I am able to recommend natural herbs, to help address physical manifestations attached to anxiety or stress you may have endured during your process of waiting.

Speak this aloud,

I renounce _______ and I no longer partner with _______ and its deceptive emotions of _______ I am free in the name of Jesus. Amen

(Example) I renounce **self-sabotage** and **insecurity** and I no longer partner with **fear** and its deceptive emotions of depression. I am free in the name of Jesus. Amen.

Maurene Burrell-Harris, MPA

3

Finding HER

"My Name Is Not My Name If It's Another Woman's"

"But daddy, how did you date someone who has the exact same name as me?" This question ran circles in my head for years as a teenager and I was compelled to ask my father in my adulthood. We were sitting in the kitchen having random conversations, reminiscing about the "good ol' days" of me growing up and concurrently of when my parents were in their youth before they arrived in the United States. My father spoke of his wild days back home in Jamaica and how he held onto that persona when he moved to the States. He spoke of the times he would drive crazy throughout the narrow dirt roads of Jamaica where he was involved in multiple accidents, some of which almost took his life. He also mentioned how he had dealt with multiple women starting at a young age. While my dad was speaking on these things, I could not help but to imagine his younger version cruising the street recklessly. I was thankful that nothing fatal happened to him during his earlier escapades. I looked at my graying father as he spoke and reminisced on his earlier years; and, in his eyes, you can see both nostalgia of him missing his youthful days and thankfulness that he is alive today to share his story.

My parents were married in Jamaica, West Indies in the month of December in the year of 1979. Little to their knowledge, just 10 years later they were going to give birth to a child in the States in the same month of their anniversary. I am often told how much of a surprise I was, although my mother had prayed to have a little girl with lots of hair. I am the youngest child maternally and paternally; and, I am also the only child of my parents to be born in the States. My dad had a bunch of children in Jamaica and I, the baby, was the one who was looked upon as "spoiled" due to the fact that my parents remained married, even to this day. I lived with both my dad and mom my entire childhood into adulthood. I found it unfortunate that my older siblings and their mothers did not have lasting relationships nor marriages. So, little ol' me who was an auntie before even being conceived was the "lucky" one who had her daddy around. You can surely say that I was a "daddy's girl" in that when I asked my dad for money to buy my youthful corner store snacks, he made the provision for me as his pockets allowed.

As we were talking, I couldn't help but to remember my childhood and all the things I endured and observed. The times I had spent with my dad in those earlier years truly shaped the person that I am today. I remember when I was about nine years old, my father brought me to an apartment building with a long hall that led to what felt like a big broad brownish-red door, which opened to a woman smiling while she greeted my daddy with a hug. I can remember being told by my dad to meet this lady who shared my name and her two daughters that were much older than me. The two girls may have been 17 and 18. My dad introduced me to the sisters and said to me, "Meet your new sisters. Go in the room and play with them," a command he gave to me since they were now my "siblings"; and, as relatives, it's natural to play with one another. I can remember the feeling I felt inside when he told my nine 9 year old self to meet my sisters. I was confused, unhappy, sad, and emotional to the point of tears as I knew that I did not want to go play with these grown girls whom I did not know from a can of paint. Nonetheless, as the good daughter I was, I listened to my father and went into the room with the sisters. I remember sitting in the room with the girls and making small talk but feeling very aware that this something was fishy about the situation because this woman and her two daughters were not my mother and my real siblings.

I remember going home to my mother, whom my dad was still married to, telling my mom about the woman and her two daughters. I remember the look on my mom's face when I told her. She was upset, but she tried her best to mask the many emotions that I've become privy to as an adult. Ideally, any woman would have concealed her true feelings when she found out her husband took her baby girl to another woman's house and told her that the woman and her children are her new family. If I were in my mother's shoes, I would have been extremely enraged, bursting with fury. But at that point of me saying these things to my mom, she did not display this anger to me. Instead, she listened while I told her about my day with the woman who bears my same name.

There was another time I remember watching my mom in the kitchen bent over on the sink. I assumed she was washing dishes because her hands were hanging over the sink. As I walked up to her, I saw tears seep down her cheek. I, being a little girl and not knowing exactly what was going on, but having some sort of idea, said to mommy, "It's going to be okay." Her despair was too heavy for my hands of consolation; but, that didn't stop me from attempting to intervene in her time of need. My daddy used to come home at night in a drunkard state. He would then start cursing some old Jamaican curses at my mommy, while they argued intensely. Suddenly, I would be interrupted by the sound of him slamming furniture and throwing things around, which was followed by a glass crack. This one particular night, after the usual rampage, I remember my daddy leaving the house speeding off fast in his car leaving a tattoo of black marks on the ground. My dad would never let his fury lead him to becoming physically violent with my mother; so, he released his frustrations on things around him.

The aforementioned time was not the only time we went to the apartment of the woman who has my name. We visited her apartment another time. But, this time I was accompanied by my brother's step-daughter, who was my best friend. She was one year older than me; and, at the age of 10, she was very aware of life and did not hold her tongue for anyone. This time in the woman's house, I remember us bringing a bag of candy, lollipops, and other snacks we had just picked up from the corner store. I opened one of the lollipops and delighted in the sweet taste of it. I was playing around with the candy in my mouth and flipped it out of my mouth as it landed on one of the woman's pictures. My friend and I laughed incredibly loudly at my unintentional, but timely gesture. During this time my dad and the woman were in the kitchen. She had just handed my dad a plate of food she made for him as he indulged in it. The woman and my dad both heard when the candy landed on the frame. The woman came over to the picture frame and said, "It's okay", but my dad, on the other hand, was so upset at us that he began to yell. "Why did you throw the lollipop at her picture?" I responded with a mere shoulder shrug, thinking that would suffice. Deep down I knew why I threw the candy on her picture. I had no respect for this woman because of the simple fact that she was not my mother — I didn't need another reason. When the woman and my dad went back into the kitchen, we resumed our comedic relief session. I felt accomplished, because in that moment I thought I destroyed something of this woman who had my daddy's heart.

My dad's back and forth fiascos with other women went on for years, despite the fact that my mother was exposed to it. I met the lady who shared my name at nine years old. As time went on, there was a change that took place in my dad's life that turned him away from the drinking, multiple women, and profuse profanity. My dad accepted Jesus Christ as his Lord and Savior of his life. I remember witnessing that special day at church. He was very emotional as he poured his heart out before God on that altar. The tears that streamed down his face made me believe that from that day forward there was going to be change in him that would finally bring his stepping out on my mother and excessive drinking to a halt. I can say from that day on my dad's relationship with God grew stronger. A few years later he became the head deacon at that very church and began working closely with the Bishop until his passing. Our Bishop left the earth in 2013 leaving behind the legacy of always having ultimate Faith through anything. This very magical lesson left a lasting impact on my father.

Childhood Memories Creep Into Adulthood

It is crazy how memories, especially suppressed childhood memories, can affect your entire life. Join me in exploring this statement a little further. The American Psychological Association's article entitled "Happy Childhood Memories Linked to Better Health Later in Life" addresses data from research of two nationally representative samples, the National Survey of Midlife Development in the United States and the Health and Retirement Study, which included over 22,000 participants in the study. The researcher, William J. Chopik PhD of Michigan State University stated, "We know that memory plays a huge part in how we make sense of the world — how we organize our past experiences and how we judge how we should act in the future. As a result, there are a lot of different ways that our memories of the past can guide us." (American Psychological Association, 2018). Dr. Chopik states that childhood memories play an important role in the development of how we as adults judge how we should act in the future. These memories that we carry deeply impact us to the point that it guides us in our decision making and how we live our lives. Childhood memories shape the adult you become.

The article at hand focuses on childhood memories as it relates to the mothers role in a child's life. It distinctly highlights the fact that research rarely examines the role fathers play in child development. (American Psychological Association, 2018). This text which emphasized the effects of mothers on children vs fathers on children piqued my interest in examining the effects fathers have on adults during child rearing age. My further studies enlightened me on how men, in particular, are directly impacted by childhood memories of their fathers. I attribute my discovery to "Childhood Memories of Father Have Lasting Impact on Men's Ability to Handle Stress." The article makes the claim that "Sons who have fond childhood memories of their fathers are more likely to be emotionally stable in the face of day-to-day stress, according to psychologists who studied hundreds of adults of all ages." Men who had active paternal presence during their formative years were more likely to become more emotionally stable. If this is the finding for a great upbringing, then men who did not have a great upbringing with their fathers are more likely to not have a balanced emotional life.

I am cognizant of the fact that the man that my father developed into is a direct reflection of his formative years. I don't view my dad as a horrible person. Men from the Caribbean often grow up with very little resources, which creates a go-hard approach when providing for their families, even if the provisions may seem minimal to some.

I believe his prior relationships with women were very interesting in the fact that he had his first child at the age of 15 years old. When I asked him to explain the reason he conceived a child at such an early age, he responded, "there was nothing else to do; there was no tv." He rendered a sly chuckle as he said this. Considering he was exposed to sex at a young age and then conceived a child, there is some form of trauma somewhere there. I never asked him, but I always wondered when he lost his virginity and was initially exposed to sex. These factors are crucial to your adulthood. Trauma and memories from childhood follow you for a lifetime, especially if you are not privy to strong coping mechanisms to help deal with the trauma. My dad coped by entertaining multiple women and fathering many children. Cognitive therapy was a taboo to my father's generation. There are so many layers of unpacking to do in order to grasp a fruitful understanding of people and their actions — not to make an excuse for it.

If this is my name, then who am I?

Toiling with the thought of my father and his mistress as my namesake caused more trauma in my life than I ever imagined. I remember a time when I did not like my name. The name "Maurene" was unattractive to me and the sound of it made me cringe internally — it actually pierced my ears. I can remember talking to my mom one day during my early teen years pleading my case to legally change my name. She questioned my intent to change my name. I remember telling her I wanted to change my name because I've never heard of anyone else that shared it. Common names of that time were more modern and I was this young girl stuck with such an old name. I really hated it. My name imprisoned me into being a person I dreaded; and, at times it left me with a sense of insecurity.

Although my name didn't touch my sweetest spots, I do remember my parents telling me the story of how they chose it. My father was a manager of a big apartment complex, where he worked with a plethora of people of diverse ethnicities. One of the ladies he worked with was an Italian lady, who helped my parents with the closing of their first home — this home is still significant as they have occupied it until this day. My father promised her that he would name his daughter after her as a sign of thanksgiving for her assistance in finding their home. And so he did.

The explanation of my name choice serves its endearing purpose — to an extent. However, it was not enough to fully counteract my annoyance with the thought of having an old person's name. This disdain led my curiosity into a frenzy, searching for the details of my name's real meaning. One day, I set out to research the meaning of my name and I found that the exact spelling of my name is one derivative of a girl's name and is Latin with the meaning of "star of the sea." Furthermore, it is a version of the name Mary. The name "Maurene" is of Irish, Gaelic descent. Essentially, since my name is derived from the name Mary, I decided to further examine what the name Mary meant. I discovered in the article written by Sara Couglin (2017) titled "Today Celebrates The Mysterious End of The Virgin Mary's Life" the name Mary, who in this article is the birth mother of Jesus, was sometimes called the first believer and she represented an exemplary Christian. She was painted as the embodiment of God's mercy, forgiving and protecting sinners regardless of their indiscretions. (Couglin, 2017).

The literal meaning of my name is, "star of the sea", of Irish descent, and it comes from the name Mary which is the manifestation of God's grace. Composed in the definitions of my name, you can see that I was not named Maurene by accident. It was ordained for me to have this name because of the destiny assigned to my life. It may have not been as obvious to me initially; but, as my life began to unfold, the veil of my name's significance was removed.

Oh She's the Homie!

My dad changed his life and outlook on relationships in his older years. Everything that I witnessed growing up shaped my outlook on relationships as I entered adulthood. The lifestyle you've become acclimated to during the nurturing stage of life, along with your parents' advice, has a way of manifesting in your own adult life, in which you begin to mirror their lifestyle. For me, I desired to explore life because I wanted my own independence. I wanted to independently attain the taste of life. I wanted to experience relationships differently from what I saw with my parents, unbeknownst to me I would experience many similarities.

Do you remember the first time you had a crush on someone? I surely remember my first crush. It was right before I entered high school. I had my eye on this boy from my neighborhood — I swore he would become my boyfriend, possibly my husband one day. I believe that in order to start dating someone who would be faithful to you, you should develop a strong friendship first — this would ensure an inevitably healthy relationship.

And that is exactly what I did. I befriended him first. Whenever this boy would come around I engaged in small talk with him and talked about different things that interested him and showed him how cool of a person I was. I honestly thought I was showing him the type of girl he should be friends with but also someone he can like too. I became his friend in hopes that our friendship would turn into more. But it did not work out that way. Instead, he just saw me as a person that was cool and fun to be around only as a friend. Little did I know, this same trend of me being a nice, loving person, only to be viewed as a friend, would last for years to come.

In high school, like many other teenagers, I had interests in several guys who I found myself befriending. I was known for playing sports, such as basketball and volleyball, year around. I enjoyed sports and my conversations made it very evident. Having a love for sports worked in my favor when it came to dating — guys loved the fact that we shared common interests. I not only shared my love for sports with them, I was also able to share common life perspectives and other random interests. If I had a gut feeling that you were a genuine potential, I shared my truest heart.

When I became vulnerable, guys viewed it as an exclusive privilege to my inner world; and, to an extent, it was. However, I eventually started to gain insight into a pattern — I was viewed as their "close friend" or "best friend" instead of girlfriend material. They often expressed their feelings for me and we would "talk" — the term we used that expressed you getting to know someone you liked or had interest in, almost dating, but not quite. During the "talking" stage I let my guard down, becoming susceptible, in hopes that it would lead to a real relationship. Unfortunately, to my dismay, it never did. I often remained in the friend zone; and, even more disheartening, I was coined as the "friend on the side" while they acquired a girlfriend, which I subsequently learned deep into their relationship, despite receiving their flirtations and heart stabbing "I love you" expressions. I despised being the "side friend" and knew deep down that I deserved more; but, I often settled because I desired love. So, I rationalized with myself that some attention was better than nothing at all.

Witnessing how much my dad's infidelity impacted my mom left me with trauma and fear of being hurt in such a way that she experienced. Yes, I love my daddy and I believe I was a daddy's girl, but I knew that I did not want to date anyone who embodied his traits of being unfaithful. Consequently, even though I deemed befriending a guy first was the best thing to do before rushing into a relationship, I realized that it was just a defense mechanism for me to protect myself from the pain of infidelity.

I developed deep rooted trust issues with men; I did not believe they had the capacity to view me as being relationship material. I desired to be loved and not be cheated on; so, I would become friends with a guy in hopes that that would not happen. I realized that despite how much diligence I invested in finding a faithful mate, guys who were the antithesis always seemed to find me.

I remember a situation I experienced in college. My cousin was preparing to marry her boyfriend of many years and she presented me with the honor of being her bridesmaid. At that time I was 20 years old; so, the idea of being a bridesmaid intrigued me. This somehow served as a right of passage into adulthood. The wedding weekend finally came around and we were all expected to join the wedding party for the festivities that would take place. My cousin advised me to catch a ride with her fiance's brother and sister who were going to the festivities, as they were also in the wedding party as a groomsman and bridesmaid. I agreed and took the ride. During the ride there were very few words between the brother and I. Let's fast forward to the wedding rehearsal. At the rehearsal, I was partnered with one of the groomsmen, who I found to be very handsome, comical, and charming. We shared similar cultural experiences, which accentuated my attraction to him. He was slightly older than me but seemed to be someone I would potentially want to spend time with outside of the wedding. I had an inkling that he was interested too.

The day of the wedding finally approached, and I can remember walking upstairs to meet the rest of the bridal party. I will not forget the amount of eyes that rested on me as I took my first step, especially from two distinct people from the groomsmen side – they were in awe. The two eye gazers were my partner, who I already developed a chemistry with, and my cousin's then soon to be brother-in-law, the one who I rode with and shared very minimal conversation with me during the ride to the wedding events.

The wedding started and as planned I walked down the aisle with my partner hand in hand. We had a great time celebrating my cousin and her new husband. As the night digressed, I noticed my partner who walked me down the aisle. We shared our goodbyes and a few inside jokes. Then I turned to walk out the door. Before I made it to the door, I ran into my cousin's brother-in-law, the one who gave me a ride. I then said my goodbyes to him as well. In doing so, I reminded him that he already had my phone number from the drive to the wedding weekend. I invited him to share it with the groomsman who I was partnered with. I gave him a big smile, hoping he would share the number, and left out the door. My thoughts traveled and I landed in instant euphoria at the idea of receiving his text or phone call. My phone rang. I noticed that it was not my partner that texted me but it was my cousin's brother-in-law. Yes, a surprise text from this guy who barely conversed with me in the car. In that text he expressed his interest in getting to know me. I was shocked but also intrigued. This one text eventually led to the next 4 years of a relationship.

Now, I will reveal every detail of this relationship in this portion, however, I will offer a snippet of our story. In the beginning there were so many butterflies — an instant connection and infatuation that easily grew into love. We went on dates and met one another's families. Our families were close through the marriage and planned a life together forever, at least that's what I thought. I had just turned 21 years old when we made it official and I was extremely excited to finally have a boyfriend. He was my first real boyfriend and proved to be completely different from the guys of my past. Seemingly, it was too good to be true, because, for the first time, a guy that I liked shared mutual feelings, expressing a desire to be my boyfriend, not just a friend with benefits.

Initially, our love rendezvous was amazing, a fairy tale, which rendered plans of marriage. This transpired within the first 6 months; but, the fairy tale suddenly began to take a shift for the worst. We made it official in December, and by June of the next year, my heart was broken. I was unsure of the person who I was with and furthermore unsure of who I was. In June, I found out that my boyfriend, whom I thought was going to be my husband, had sexual relations with his ex-girlfriend in his dorm room months before in February. I found out about this through a social media direct message from the friend of his ex-girlfriend. Yes, his ex-girlfriend's friend told me that my then boyfriend cheated on me. At first I was in disbelief; but, I still decided to confront him. When I did, he was speechless — seemingly white as a ghost. It was horrifying, the biggest pain I ever felt in my life. My grief led me to cut ties with him for a few weeks. I demanded that he leave me alone.

During those weeks of being apart, I encountered many of my deep rooted insecurities that I buried previously. I felt as though I wasn't good enough, pretty enough, or skinny enough. These insecurities first inhabited my mind in my younger years when I noticed that guys were only interested in being connected with me as a friend. In this circumstance, the thoughts appeared once again because of his infidelity. Despite how angry I was that he cheated and knew that it was his fault for cheating, I still found myself taking some of the blame for his indiscretion due to my insecurities.

During the time of us not speaking to one another, my ex reached out to me on every social media platform. He even dedicated songs to me and sent flowers, showering me with "love" so intensely, that I convinced myself I could forgive him and that we could work on our relationship. So I ended up taking him back into my heart. I rationalized this with his persistence and remorse for my situation.

I took him back but it did not mean the hurt and pain completely dissipated. My insecurities became bigger and I often found myself comparing myself to other women whom he said were his friends. My ex was a popular party promoter; and, with that came many women in and out of our lives. I dealt with those women for a few years and my insecurities continued to swell as I compared myself to these women. We eventually broke up and it wasn't because I decided to break the bond. It was actually my ex who tried to convince me that I was concentrating on him too much and needed to focus on myself. He believed that it was best that we went our separate ways. Sadly, this communication transpired as a phone conversation. Yes, a phone conversation was how we started and how we ended.

I did not realize there was a true meaning behind my desire to become friends with guys I dated before they became a boyfriend until now. The rationale for this is because of trust issues with men, stemming from the relationships of my dad. I did not trust that a guy would be faithful to me so it would be better to be friends with them first to build some sort of a bond would be unscathed. Friends are not supposed to deceive friends, right? I learned in my last relationship that, although being friends is a beautiful thing, which is definitely helpful in any relationship, being friends first did not matter, because ultimately the outcome isn't predicated on establishing friendship initially. The only thing that mattered was if two individuals in the relationship are committed to one another wholeheartedly.

My Name in Christ!

Throughout this chapter, I shared what I thought my name meant based on the name that I was given at birth, the name of the other woman, how others viewed me, and the name that I always wanted to become: girlfriend. As I grew into adulthood, I realized that the "name" others saw me as was not the name that truly defines me. My name in Christ is the name that matters the most and is the name that I function in.

When the break up with my ex occurred, it left me distraught, battling with many emotions and insecurities. I found myself contemplating where we went wrong and playing the blame. My pain put up a veil, disguising my real identity from me. This break up brought me to one of the lowest places in my life. Hearing him utter "you're focusing too much on me and not enough on yourself" pierced the core of my being. It penetrated my heart so intensely because it was a harsh reality; and, encountering the truth can sting. I was spending way too much time during our relationship focused on his whereabouts, if he really loved me, if he would cheat again, etc. Being consumed with the idea of him dealing with numerous women snatched my focus of the essence of who I was and whose I was, and ultimately hindered my relationship with God.

The break up broke me, but it did not keep me broken. Through-out my childhood, I was very active in my church and developed a relationship with Christ from a young age. I remember the first time I went to the altar, at the age of 11, and gave my life to Christ. Although I accepted salvation at 11, my teenage and early adult years were filled with youthful lust. Nonetheless, my relationship with God was still intact, to a degree. The break up, even in bringing me to one of the lowest places in life, was one of the best things that happened to me as it allowed me to become reacclimated to the love that I originally had with My Heavenly Father, God.

To my Heavenly Father, I am more than a friend and more than just my "birth" name. I am His masterpiece created in His own image according to Ephesians 2:10. I am of royal priesthood and peculiar people according to 1 Peter 2:9. I am the righteousness of God according to 2 Corinthians 5:21. I am a child of God according to John 1:12. I am chosen according to 1 Thessalonians 1:4. I am accepted according to Romans 15:7. I am complete in Him according to Colossians 2:10. I am complete. No missteps were made when my God made me. When He made me He looked at His creation and saw that it was very good. My Heavenly Father gave me a new name that is in alignment with His biblical truths because he loved me unconditionally. I am His daughter. The love of my Abba Father is greater than any person in this world.

What God says about me is what matters. This relationship with My Heavenly Father is the utmost important relationship that, I now know, I need to cater to first and foremost. This premier relationship will then add value to the surrounding finite relations here on earth. I will no longer allow myself to forget who and whose I Am.

I realize that my proclamation of my dad in the beginning of this chapter may paint a less than favorable picture of him; but, I am compelled to make this declaration: he is not a horrible man. I believe he was just lost and was unfortunately living a life without consequences. The hurt he left my mother and family with was painful for us at the time. However, now that he is much older, I am sure he reflects on his wild days and finds remorse. I've often overheard my dad on the phone with his friends, discussing his terrible failures as a husband. He highlights my mom for being a strong, supportive, resilient wife and mother. He realizes that he could not develop into the man he eventually amounted to without her – a very good life lesson learned.

I am someone who has become familiar with myself and my strength as a woman. I am not perfect, nor do I try to become someone who is perfect. The only perfect person to ever exist on this earth was Jesus Christ. I know I can strive to be like Jesus, but I will never be Him. I always believe in being the realist version of yourself. I always believe in being truly transparent. So, holding true to my value of transparency, I walk in honesty. Writing this chapter was a tedious task. I wanted to give up so many times. I thought about how me telling my story would affect my parents, who are still married to this day. I worried about how my parents and the rest of my family would feel about telling a story about our past. I was afraid to open my mouth out of fear. But I had to write this chapter. I had to get my story out for that little girl who was stuck in not truly knowing who she is and her worth as a woman. I am a daddy's girl to God, my Father in Heaven, and also to my biological dad here on earth.

Daddy and mommy, I love you both. I hope you're not upset with this. But I know that writing was imperative to my sanity. I wrestled with myself many times while writing this. Frustration attempted to cripple me to the point of not writing this but I had to do it. It is for my healing – and it is for your healing. Accept this as my gift of healing to you.

Steps To Live By:

- Be comfortable in your skin.
- Do your research before fully investing in someone of interest.
- Allow God to fix YOU, before presenting yourself to your mate. You don't have to appear perfect; but, a healed version of yourself is more valuable than a broken version.

Jacquelyn Wilson

4

Worth the Weight

From Prisoner to Princess

Disney is a billion-dollar company that is known for a plethora of creative works and products; however, one of the most recognizable aspects of their brand is the "Disney Princess." Cinderella is the princess I have always connected and identified with, primarily because her whole world shifted after she lost her dad. She experienced bondage at the hand of her stepmom and stepsisters, but she did not let her circumstantial plight distract her from her purpose. Once she realized she had supernatural resources at her avail, she became the princess she was destined to be!

Like Cinderella, my dad was my first love, and ironically, his nickname for me was "Princess." That sobriquet was appropriate since he treated me as such. He passionately provided my every need and cared for my heart with intentionality, and through him I experienced the gravity of unconditional love at an early age. My dad was the prototype for the man I was willing to wait a lifetime for, but unfortunately, he passed away when I was eleven.

As painful as my dad's death was, it was not my first traumatic experience. When I was nine, I was raped by a family friend, and I literally felt my innocence die that day! The little princess that fantasized about rainbows and unicorns had a rude awakening about the intricacies of real life. Just as Cinderella experienced the chains of oppression that her pseudo family attempted to place upon her, I too wrestled with the weighty chains of unworthiness, abandonment, shame, and low self-worth.

Shortly after the passing of my dad, my mom's distressing grief led her to drug addiction and less than a year later my sister and I were taken away from her and placed in the care of my aunt. My two brothers, who were older, were left in my mom's care. Thus, causing my sister and I to be separated from our siblings.

My life was forever changed by other people's decisions, and over time I began to feel imprisoned by my own thoughts, fears and insecurities. Yet, I did not let my prison dictate my perspective. The truth is God will use your pain to propel you into your purpose, and no matter what you've experienced in life, it is possible to rise above it and allow God to turn your trauma into triumph!

From Traumatized to Triumphant
Life experiences that are deeply disturbing can traumatize a person. The American Psychological Association (APA) describes trauma as

"an emotional response to a terrible event like an accident, rape, or natural disaster." When someone experiences trauma, they will have a *fight or flight response,* which basically means if they are in danger, they will either fight or run. This is an automatic response that happens to everyone who finds themselves in a frightening circumstance, and one's body pumps adrenaline and other chemicals during this response.

When someone who has experienced trauma does not go through the normal cycle of healing, they run the risk of getting stuck in a fight or flight response cycle. This is called "fight or flight freeze." Those stuck in this state experience the same symptoms as soldiers diagnosed with PTSD. People who find themselves in this state for long periods of time eventually feel numb and they dissociate. Dissociation is a mental process where a person disconnects from their thoughts, feelings, memories, and sense of identity. Another indication that someone is not healed from their trauma is they are easily triggered.

I never received the healing necessary to move on from my past traumas, so I found myself dissociating from everyone around me and I was easily triggered by various people, places, and things that reminded me of my past. My broken family situation made me desire a family of my own. I wanted a "normal" family that could give me the love I felt I deserved. Thus, out of my desperate need for affection and attention, I began to look for love and validation in all the wrong places which left me more broken, confused, numb, and imprisoned!

The story of Cinderella is very reminiscent of my story. She too was left traumatized by life's unexpected and uncontrollable twists and turns. The loss of her mom caused her dad to eventually remarry because he wanted a mother figure to raise her. However, before this new family unit could get acclimated to their new reality, her dad passes away too. This tragic event left Cinderella at the mercy of her stepmother and step-sisters, who all had impure intentions toward her. These sinister relatives that are now responsible for loving and caring for her decided to treat her like a slave instead, and the home she once considered as a place of joy and fond memories was now her prison.

Most of you are familiar with this extraordinary story of how Cinderella overcame her trauma through the assistance of strangers. Sometimes the people we expect to assist us through life's hardships are those who let us down, and it takes outside assistance to get us to where we are supposed to end up. For Cinderella, it took the aid of her fairy godmother, prince charming, and some other noteworthy characters to get her to her destiny.

Similarly, I overcame my trauma through the help of sources outside of my birth family. First and foremost, I found the love, validation, safety, and stability I needed through my relationship with Jesus Christ. Once I learned who God is and who I am in Him, the yokes that weighed me down began to break! Also, prayer, learning the Word of God, and several counselors over the years helped me find my true self. Through counseling, I learned to process my pain instead of running from it; and, I learned how to forgive those who hurt me just as God forgave me.

If you're reading this and my story resonates with you, it is imperative that you let go of any unforgiveness, resentment and/or bitterness you may feel toward those who hurt you and release them to God. Your triumph is indicative of you healing properly and moving on from the things in your past that have a hold on you. Once you heal, you are in a better position to believe and receive all the wonderful promises that God has waiting for you!

From Woman in Waiting to Wife

Most people in our culture do not have to wait long to travel, enjoy a meal, access a movie, or talk to a loved one. Technologies such as planes, microwaves, the internet, and cell phones, have made life extremely convenient for those of us in developed countries. Such inventions make processes faster and more efficient, which makes our lives easier to navigate and more enjoyable. However, the advancement of technology has also created a generation of people who have very little patience when it comes to waiting.

This can be problematic because there are certain things in life like marriage, having children, overcoming sickness, etc., that are out of our locus of control. Therefore, we have no choice but to wait on God's appointed time for those types of specific things in our life to unfold. Patience is a virtue and there is a season for everything under the sun. Yet the challenge for most of us is giving God full control of our lives.

I have always had a desire in my heart to get married and have children, but I never would have imagined an eighteen-year gap between the time that I thought I was ready for marriage and when I said, "I Do." In my mind I was prepared for marriage at the age of 24. That was when I fully submitted my life to Christ and made a commitment to do things God's way by committing to not having sex before marriage. I practiced celibacy for four years after receiving Jesus as the Lord and Savior of my life, but my faith began to waver after getting closer to the age of 30 because like most women, I had a timeline in my head for marriage.

I imagined myself being married no later than thirty. So, my patience and faith began to be tested when God's will for my life did not line up with my life's plans. Although I had victory over my flesh for four years, I did what many weary Christians do. I stepped outside of God's will and gave into temptation.

I started dating someone whose values did not line up with mine, and after several months of him pressuring me to have sex, I compromised my moral stance. This created what many Christians call a *soul tie* and in an instance one bad decision robbed me of the power I maintained for years.

I became weak and unable to say "no" to sexual sin, and although I would love to say I quickly broke off the relationship, that is not true. I struggled on and off with that toxic relationship for many years. I eventually stopped going to church because of the shame and condemnation, and a woman that was once free in Christ became bound again!

I eventually got engaged to the guy who tempted me in my fall from grace, but after a few months of being engaged, I began to seek God again and get back in church. I soon realized that the man I was engaged to was not the right mate for me, so I quickly broke off the relationship. I recommitted my mind, body, soul, and spirit back to Christ and I vowed to never compromise my morals again or to be unequally yoked with someone who was the antithesis of who I am!

One thing that I have learned about God is sometimes He prefers for us to take the scenic route because He is all-knowing and sees our end from the beginning. In fact, God planned our whole lives before we were in our mother's womb and what he has in mind for us is superior to our plans for ourselves.

Isaiah 55:8-9 says, "For My thoughts *are* not your thoughts, nor *are* your ways My ways," says the Lord. For *as* the heavens are higher than the earth, so are My ways higher than your ways, and My thoughts than your thoughts." We may think we know what is best for our lives and perceive we are ready for the promises of God, but ultimately God knows best, and his timing is perfect! He does not prolong our blessings to punish us or to make us suffer, but to develop our character so that we are mature enough to not mishandle the blessings he has for us. The Biblical character that is a great example of this is Joseph.

Joseph was a man of outstanding character and he stayed content despite his circumstances. He also never compromised his convictions when faced with temptation. Another characteristic that set Joseph apart is his ability to forgive those who intentionally harmed him. He says to his enemies, who happen to be his brother, in Genesis 50:20, "You intended to harm me, but God intended it for good to accomplish what is now being done, the saving of many lives."

The Bible lays out the story of Joseph in Genesis chapters 37 – 50. The following is a short synopsis of his story. Jacob had 12 sons, and his youngest son is Joseph. Jacob loved Joseph more than his other children, which caused his brothers to hate him. When Joseph was a young man, he had two dreams about his family bowing down to him. So, Joseph excitedly told his family about the dreams, and it made his brothers resent him even more.

One day when Joseph and his brothers were away from home in a field, they plotted to kill him. However, his oldest brother interjected and told them to throw Joseph in a well instead. They ultimately decided to sell him into slavery and pretend he was killed by a wild animal. Their dad was devastated at the news.

Joseph finds himself as a slave in Egypt because of the jealously and betrayal of his brothers. Yet, he succeeds in everything he does because of the favor of God in his life. Potiphar, his master, noticed his great leadership abilities, and therefore appointed him to oversee his household. Joseph's life suddenly takes an unexpected turn when Potiphar's wife began to lust after him and falsely accused him of rape because he rejected her advancements. Those accusations landed him in prison, but he was eventually released because of his God-given ability to interpret dreams.

Pharaoh, the King of Egypt, had a disturbing dream, and Joseph was recommended as a capable interpreter. His interpretation of Pharaoh's dream included the foretelling of a famine that would devastate many, but it also included a brilliant strategy that would minimize the impact of the famine. Pharaoh was so impressed with Joseph that he entrusted him to govern all the affairs of Egypt, and in an instance, he progressed from a prisoner to second in command. He immediately implemented the strategy God gave him and because of it several nations were saved.

Joseph's family was forced to go to Egypt to survive the famine, and when they discovered that their brother was the governor of that nation, they feared for their lives. However, Joseph had no plans to retaliate against his brothers because he saw purpose in everything that he endured, and he realized that if it were not for the series of events that transpired throughout his life, he would have not been afforded the opportunity to acquiesce to the notoriety that he received. Joseph had to wait 13 years from the time God gave him the dreams until the time he reigned as governor, but I'm convinced all the pain, disappointment, and betrayal he faced was well worth it once he saw the outcome of God's plans.

I feel the same way about my 18-year wait for my spouse. Not only was it worth the wait, but it was worth the *weight.* In other words, everything I've experienced, the rape, the death of my dad, being taken away from my mom, the heartaches in past relationships, proved to be worth going through because of the joy granted to me in marriage! Every relationship that robbed me of my identity, self-esteem, and innocence, is all worth it in retrospect.

Essentially, it is not the marriage itself that brings me joy. It is my husband! He is everything that I need in a spouse, and we balance each other perfectly. I am now cognizant of how important it is to ensure that your mate is "equally yoked" with you — Be certain that your core beliefs and values, life's goals, and temperaments align in a harmonious way.

My husband and I met at church through a mutual friend. We decided to build a six-month platonic friendship and truly took our time and got to know each other. The foundation of our marriage is Jesus Christ first and then our friendship. When someone's spouse is their best friend: they are less critical of them, and they can converse without judgment. I have truly found my prince charming like Cinderella; and, although I had to wait on my promise like Joseph, my life's experiences helped prepare me for anything my husband and I may face in the future.

There are so many scriptural references, which reverberate the importance of waiting. Isaiah 40:31 says, "But those who wait on the Lord shall renew their strength. They shall mount up with wings like eagles, they shall run and not be weary, they shall walk and not faint." Another empowering scripture about waiting is Galatians 6:9, "And let us not be weary in well doing: for in due season, we shall reap if we faint not."

So, I encourage you to not give up on your dreams despite your age, stage, or season in life! Trust God's plans and His character above your crisis! "Trust in the Lord with all your heart and lean not on your own understanding. In all your ways acknowledge him, and he shall direct your path" (Proverbs 3:5-6). Be intentional about cultivating the level of patience you need to wait on your promise, and most importantly do not compromise who you are for temporary results that do not line up with what you ultimately desire!

Strategies While Waiting

1. Develop a personal relationship with God and heal from past traumas through:

   ○ Committing yourself to prayer and fasting.
   ○ Studying the Bible as a guide for your everyday life.
   ○ Worshiping God and learning how to hear his voice.
   ○ Seeking a professional counselor if needed.

2. Discover who you are as an individual before marriage through learning what you:

- Believe.
- Need and want in a partner.
- Are passionate about and destined to do.
- Enjoy for self-care and fun.

3. Establish a safe community of family, friends, and mentors to:

- Safeguard you from pitfalls like loneliness and isolation.
- Keep you accountable.
- Provide you with love, encouragement, support, motivation, guidance, and correction.

Makeni Williams

5

The Bridge

Preparation

Preparation is defined as setting things in order for something that is to come. How long will it take before the fruit is manifested? A person decides they want to become fit so they purchase a gym membership. They go to the gym daily to follow that exercise regime that has been prepared. The person needs to go to the gym three to five times weekly in preparation for the desired result. Depending on the time spent at the gym and the amount of work put in, will determine how long it will take you to achieve the desired result.

The preparation for me was not quite that simple. I had to be tried and tested in the fire. Disobedience caused a delay of the process. I was known to choose the wrong men. Controlling, abusive men were my claim to fame. My first boyfriend was very disrespectful to me. He played on my naivete and lack of self confidence to control me. He succeeded until I grew tired.

The next one had the pleasure of spending ten of the best years of my life with me. He abused drugs (crack was his drug of choice). I did not know about this. My lack of street knowledge did not allow me to realize this was occurring until I saw him coming out of the neighborhood crack house. By this time, he had stolen every piece of jewelry that I owned, drained my bank account, and abused me physically, mentally, and emotionally. I thought that I loved this man more than life itself. Then one day I had an epiphany. Why was I allowing this man to hurt me over and over again? Do you believe this is love? I remember waking up one morning and saying to myself, "Today is the day that I am ending this tumultuous roller coaster ride and moving on." I prayed to God to not allow him to beat me or hurt me in any way. He actually got on his knees and cried. I could care less. I was over it!!!!!!!!!!

On to my next adventure on the rebound drew another addict — one who sniffed heroin. He tormented me emotionally and mentally. The cycle was not breaking. It was a perpetual cycle of abuse — over and over again. Like a merry go round. I was tired but obviously I was not tired enough. I wanted a man who was tall, dark and handsome. I wanted a man who turned the heads of women as we walked into a restaurant. I still did not accept the fact that the superficial qualities that I was pursuing in a man were causing me pain, grief and suffering. The reason was because their spirits were in torment.

So the struggle continued, I went from one man after another who were full of insecurities: addicts, womanizers, controllers, abusers, deceivers. I kept saying, "This is the one right here." This is what I said every time I met a loser. My spirit was drawing these losers. My pastor told me that I needed to figure out what was in my spirit that was allowing me to keep attracting the same type of men.

Throughout those 30 years, there were many tumultuous relationships. I went from one dysfunctional situation to another. The straw that broke the camel's back was when I met a man who not only possessed all of those toxic traits that I was attracted to, but he was also a psycho/sociopath literally!!! He tried to kill me by choking me, killed my cat, and traumatized my family. At the age of 51, I grew REALLY TIRED of the dating scene. I fell prostrate before the Lord and cried. I cried for hours. The Lord spoke to me and said, "Daughter, you need to change your perception of what you consider a good man." If you start looking at the inner qualities of the man from the inception, then God will bless you with a man who genuinely loves you."

I was not sure what that would entail nor was I able to comprehend what thus saith the Lord at that time, but one thing I did know was that God would reveal His plan for my life. I had to go through this stage in life so I could be prepared for that which was to come. I had to go through the process of the preparation phase so I could appreciate my future blessing.

The Training Ground

After 30 years of going through the preparation phase, a sister was exhausted and depleted. What's next? I was scared to ask that question though, for fear of what could really be next. I could not fathom what the Lord had in store for me in this next phase of my life. It was something that I never expected.

After almost losing my life while seeking love in all the wrong places, I came to the conclusion that it was God's plight and plan for my life to be a single woman. I was going to continue enjoying my life, doing the things that I want to do, like traveling the world, engaging in

African dancing, enjoying fine dining, and spending quality time with family and friends. I was not going to allow the enemy to make me believe that I was doomed because I did not have a husband. I was going to practice what the scripture says in Philippians 4:11, I have learned in whatsoever state in, I am going to be content.

I went on my 12th Festival at Sea Cruise with 4 of my friends. Festival at Sea is an all-black cruise sponsored by Blue World Travel so you know it is a party all day and night. My intention was to have a good time without thinking about my relationship status. 2 days before disembarkation, while getting my lunch on the lido deck, I was introduced to a man: a man that would change the way that I viewed men forever. His name was Mr. B.

Mr. B was indeed different from any man that I ever had. I was introduced to him by his friend and I smiled and kept it moving. The next day while engaging in a line dance session, Mr. B spotted me and joined the class. We actually had a conversation and he asked me to attend the comedy show with him. This was our first date. He treated me like a lady — so kind, a gentle giant. I was not accustomed to this kind of treatment. We exchanged numbers and decided to keep in touch. I thought to myself, "Makeni, here you go again." Deep down inside I knew that I would not stick around if I saw that this relationship was not right for me.

Mr. B and I established a relationship after the second date. I knew that this man was different from the others; however, I was still apprehensive, unsure, and afraid. The cruise was over and now it was back to reality. Is this his vacation persona or is this who he is? Drama ensued one month after we met. The drama was not from him, though, but from the deranged sociopath, whom I had broken up with 4 months before. He began stalking and harassing me when I refused to answer his phone calls. I did not realize that he had been following me also. He came to my house one morning after I worked a night shift. He dragged me on the floor, beat me, tried to choke me, and knocked me out. Mr. B was away at the time assisting a friend with a cross country move. When Mr. B heard the news, he came back on the next flight to New York to be by my side. I was expecting him to jump ship and figuring that he did not want to stick around because he would fear for his own life. That was not the case at all. This is when the confirmation came that this man really cares about me. No other man had ever gone out of their way to assist me when I was down.

Mr. B took me into his home and our relationship progressed to a deeper level. He helped to save me from torment and destruction. After facing a near death experience, my life drastically changed for the better. Hence, from the day after that horrible situation, I titled it, "The first day of the rest of my life." We did everything together from traveling, to attending cultural events, parties with family and friends, etc. This was real love and I was finally gripping it. 2 ½ years of sheer bliss and true unconditional love came to an abrupt ending. The Lord called Mr. B home to glory. It was one of the saddest days of my life. I questioned God because I did not understand. I asked the Lord, "Why would He give me love, after all of the trials and tribulations that I've been through and take it away from me?"

Once again , here I am sad, destitute, and depressed. I became angry at God and did not understand what God wanted me to learn from this. I was the happiest I had ever been in my life in a relationship, and, in the twinkling of an eye, the tables turned. I did not know that this was my training ground.

The Result of the Wait

While sitting in my lonely apartment pondering over my life for the past 3 years, a divine revelation came to me. God informed me that this apartment was a bridge. Bridge to what? Where? What do you mean Lord? I got bored and lonely in my small apartment and I decided that I was ready to date again to help me move past my depressed state so I went on a dating site. I was apprehensive about this at first, but I decided that I would give it a try. "There has to be a man out there in my age range looking for a decent woman to spend the rest of his life with also. I started out meeting losers; however, because of my experience with Mr. B, I knew what love looked like and I was not settling for less. I met several losers and quickly kicked them to the curb. (And guess what?) It felt really good doing it. As soon as I was ready to leave it alone and go back to my single contentment, so to speak, I met my soulmate, my husband, my Boaz.

The Duke and I were both at a point in life where we were ready for true commitment. On our first date, we realized that we had several things in common. We both enjoyed old school music, had close ties to our family, and desired to spend our lives with someone we can travel the world with. We talked about our parents on a daily basis keeping their spirits alive in our hearts.

The Duke and I met in October; and, 5 months later, the pandemic happened. I did not know exactly how long we would be on a curfew but I knew that I did not want to sit in that small apartment alone for God knows how long. I called The Duke and asked him if he mind having a house guest during the pandemic and he quickly replied, "No, I don't mind, come on." I packed my bags and went on my way. I knew that this would either make us or break us. My father always said, "Live with me ain't like come see me." Time will tell.

We both came into each other's life at the right time. Shortly after we met, The Duke developed an arrhythmia from the many years of stress that he encountered. I discovered the arrhythmia and insisted that he go to his doctor that day. He listened. His arrhythmia is now being controlled. He tells everyone that I saved his life. He, in turn, saved my life because I was in a dark place and had a hard time shaking it. The Duke coming into my life, brought me to see the light again. I was happy again. God blessed me with true love once again, even after I doubted him — true love not once, but twice, in my fifties.

We became engaged 13 months into the relationship and 22 months later we were joined together in holy matrimony. Look at God!!!!!! I never in a million years thought that I would get married at this age. I am 59 years old and married for the first time. Married to a man, who truly loves me for me. We are perfect for one another. God carved us out to be together at this time in our lives to enjoy the rest of our years together. We do everything together, He is my best friend. We enjoy one another so much. All of the years of hurt, pain, and sorrow has paid off. I give God all of the glory, honor, and praise. It was a long, hard road; but, the end result was worth waiting for. I have no regrets.

As you can see, I had a long tiring dating experience. Due to my disobedience, I had to go through the school of hard knocks. God gave me revelation every time I was in an unfavorable relationship. However, I didn't take heed because I wanted what I wanted. I have a message for all of my single ladies of all ages. Psalm 37:4 states, "If you wait on the Lord He will give you the desires of your heart." Don't try to do it your way. Don't rely on what you think is "your type." When I figured out that my type was not the type that was right for me, I started to win. God gave me the desires of my heart. God gave me love, peace, and joy. The sorrows and heartaches were eliminated.

God can bless you with love at any age. I was 59 years old when I found my knight in shining armor. It's never too late. Some are blessed at a young age and others take more time. If He did it for me, He can do it for you. Don't give up!!!! I woke up every morning thanking God for blessing me with my divine mate. I spoke it daily. Through all of my disobedience, God still saw fit to bless me. It came right on time. Whether you are 25, 50, 75 or 90, it's never too late for God to bless you with your divine mate.

Steps to Live By:

- Patience is not your enemy; it is your friend.
- Know the value you possess, rather than allowing someone else to define it for you.
- Work your weight. Applied pressure can be tedious; but, without pain, there is no real gain. In your waiting season, allow the weight to build your muscle of virtue. You are a virtuous woman. Flex like you are.

Jamillah Yancey

6

W 2

I remember meeting my biological father for the first time when I was about five or six years old. I was in line at one of my favorite fast food restaurants, White Castle, with my mother. In line with us, there was a really tall, hairy, light skinned man looking down at me. I remember my mom saying to me, "Jamillah, that man over there is your father." With an astonished disposition, I began staring at him, not sure if I should speak to him or wait patiently for him to introduce himself to me. As he noticed my state of amazement, he made the first move and spoke to me. To this day, I don't remember what he actually said to me; but, one thing is for sure, I know I will never forget that moment.

I didn't see him anymore until years later when my brother and I were in foster care. My mother went through a rough period in her life that prevented her from being able to properly care for my brother and I. I was about 12 years old. During this time my brother and I had been in foster care for about two years and our caseworker worked tirelessly to find a permanent home for us. Thus, they started looking for family members who might want to take the responsibility.

Adoption was also an option. This is when the guy I was introduced to as my father resurfaced. I was reintroduced to him, but this time I met his wife and children as well. I learned I had one sister and four brothers. This is where I met my father again. At that point, I had visitation. He and his wife were willing to take both my brother and I into their home. My brother and I would visit their home. My father and step mom's home was huge, warm, and loving. I loved the fact that they had a huge family. I now had a host of siblings. It was new for us. My brother and I only had one another for so long prior to this. We loved going over to their house and hanging out. It was like a home away from home.

As much as I enjoyed going over and spending time with my new family, I did not want to go to live with them. I thought I was where I was supposed to be. God blessed me with another mother and father who raised my brother and I. With them, I felt extremely safe and loved. My parents always made me feel like I was their biological child. My father was a prestigious man in our community. He was a pastor and an entrepreneur, a barbershop owner. His strong teachings and morals molded me into the woman I am today. I say this because I remember him being a spiritually rooted man of God through his actions.

He was a man who believed in consistency. It didn't matter whether he was at church, at the barbershop, at home, or on the streets. He was known for being a beacon of light, leading people to God. I admired that about him because it showed strength, courage, and boldness. His faith was like a light from God that made me want to follow, believe, and trust him. As his daughter, this was important because I observed his genuine consistency with us, his family, as well as with others he encountered, even strangers. He was no Dr. Jekyll and Mr. Hyde type of guy. He showed the same kind of love and generosity at all times. He would give his last, even when it wasn't convenient to do so. I saw him sacrifice over and over to help many people.

Everybody in the neighborhood knew my father was a God-fearing and trustworthy man. He and my mom would drive miles away countless times to deliver food to families in need. He would also go to the shelter across the street from the church and invite everyone over to eat. I also remember my dad as a husband who embodied the perfect balance of being strong and gentle. I saw him love, respect, and be a great provider. He took care of the household, so much so that my mother was afforded the opportunity to not have to work a 9-5. I never saw him raise his voice or call her out of her name. He always treated her with respect. It made me feel safe and I realized that's how a man should treat a woman.

My parents were God-fearing and strict. Bottom line, my parents preached "no sex before marriage." They didn't deep dive into conversations about what that looked like or what to expect — it was just "no sex before marriage!" I remember my first so-called cute crush boyfriend in high school. My so-called boyfriend came over to the house and all of us were sitting on plastic covered sofas watching TV with very few words spoken. My parents eyed us like hawks. When it was time for him to go home, I walked him out to the front porch and my mother strongly objected to that; so, she prompted me to come back into the house. She said, "He doesn't need you to wait with him."

Clearly, my parents did not have the traditional birds and bees conversation about dating before marriage, which affected me in my first marriage. I was obedient until the age of 27. Against their teachings, I ended up having sex before marriage. I became pregnant. Then, we married one another when I was four months pregnant, moved in together, and had our baby. Everything expedited. Within less than a year my life completely changed.

The more and more we developed as a family, I started to see his true nature uncovered — he was nothing like my father or who I envisioned my husband would be. I experienced excessive verbal abuse that was leading to physical aggression. During our nine month marriage, on three different occasions, I experienced physical aggression that almost became violent. I remember when my son was about 3 weeks old and we got into an argument. During this time he pushed me while I was holding our son in my arms. Thank God I was standing near our bed. So, I had the bed there to break my fall.

Another incident I remember is when my son was 6 weeks old. This was my first day back to work returning from my maternity leave. I've always had a car but at this particular time I did not, because my car had been recently stolen in front of our house. My husband's car at the time had been repossessed. We had a newborn baby. We both were without a car. We had to walk to drop off our baby to my aunt's house; and, then, catch public transportation to work. I remember how cold the walk was and it wasn't even winter; but, what made it so cold was the way I was treated. I remember my son's father being angry and lashing out at me. He became enraged and as I was pushing my son in his stroller he snatched the stroller out of my hands and pushed my son until we made it to my aunt's house. When we made it to my aunt's house. I retrieved the stroller and my son and walked into my aunt's house and closed the door. I remember how upset I was and when my aunt saw my face she immediately said to me, "What's wrong Mil?" I was upset and remember crying. My aunt went into protection mode to protect me. She quickly opened the door and blurted some words to my son's father. He left and I waited to get myself together until I was able to leave for work.

After this incident, I did not return home. I stayed with my sister for a while. A few weeks later, I went back home. By the time my son was 3 months old, I refused to take the abuse anymore. The last and final straw for me was when my ex-husband came to pick me up from work one day. I remember getting into the car and leaning over to give him a kiss. Only I was met with disgust. He just looked at me as if I were a stranger. So, I leaned back into my seat. The ride home was very cold. We did not speak. I went to change the radio station to a popular talk show and I remember him saying I don't want to listen to that garbage and immediately changed the station.

Once we were off the highway and on Liberty Ave, he slammed the gear into park in the middle of the street, snatched his keys out of the ignition, jumped out of the car, and walked home. I was stunned and confused by his behavior. I was embarrassed and ashamed that I was just left to fend for myself. I got out of the car and jumped into the driver's seat. I went to pick up my son from his grandmother and aunt's house. I was done with the disrespect and abuse. Once I returned home with my son, I gathered my things, called my dad, and asked him to come pick me up.

Every time these altercations occurred, I reached out to my father. My father was my rock and protector. He was there to rescue me from what could have been a violent outcome with my husband. After I left, he would call me numerous times; and, when I didn't answer, I was left with many messages of him calling me out of my name. I was every "B" word you can think of. If I was at church, he would pop up there and wait at the end of the street. He would stalk me and make threats to my family members as well. He called my job so much that my supervisors were concerned and I thought that I may lose my job. Thank God it was just the opposite. I received nothing but support. Being concerned for my safety, I decided to file for a restraining order. This all happened before our divorce was final. This was not my idea of a marriage, especially after what I saw with my parents. I then had to learn how to be a single parent with the support of my parents for the next three years.

MOVING ON

Unbeknownst to me, I purchased a car that basically was a lemon. My father, who knew everyone in the neighborhood, introduced me to my future husband. He was the community mechanic that everybody took their car to for mechanical repairs. In the midst of his trying to repair my lemon, he expressed interest in me. I told him he was too old for me because of the 12 year difference. I didn't see myself dating someone that much older than me. However, he demonstrated several qualities like my father. He was caring, nurturing, thoughtful, protective, and a good father to his kids. More importantly, he shared a genuine interest in my three-year-old son.

Due to my broken marriage, I was hesitant but drawn to the mechanic because he had a good heart and he meant well, just like my dad. He knew my dad liked to eat at buffets. So, he decided to take me and my parents out to eat to ask permission to pursue dating me, since he regarded my parents highly.

He was a typical mechanic, whose day to day wardrobe consisted of Timbs, jeans, a work shirt, and a Yankees baseball cap. However, for this occasion, he cleaned up to impress my parents. He wore a white dress shirt, black dress pants, and black dress shoes. My parents were not impressed. They had poker faces. On the other hand, my reaction was a little different. When he arrived, I asked, "Huh, what do you have on?" I was shocked and impressed that he took the effort to impress my parents. I appreciated the level of respect he had for my parents. From there, I decided to really date the mechanic, which led to us becoming married two years later.

Three months after we married, unexpectedly, his health began to deteriorate. He had a massive heart attack and with other health complications. His health progressively grew worse. Between numerous trips to the hospital, working two jobs, caring for our kids, and taking care of my biological mother, who also became ill at that time, I became extremely overwhelmed. However, I began to put my faith in God to help maneuver these trials. Thus, through what felt like something unbearable for me to bear, God gave me strength.

Several years went by as I assisted my husband through his declining health. Fast forward, 4 years ago the unthinkable happened. My father got into a fatal car wreck that caused him to go into a coma, which led to his death a month later. Two days later, after my father's fatal car accident, my husband was rushed into intensive care due to heart issues. A month later, the man that I knew as my rock was no longer here. This loss was devastating, to say the least. I endured pain I never experienced before mixed with emptiness, depression, and a lack of hope. I was at a loss without my father, who I could always count on; he was no longer there to rescue me.

This was the beginning of me losing the three most important people of my life. A year later, I lost my mother to cancer; and, five months after she passed, I lost my husband, now faced with being a widow, single mother, working two jobs, taking care of my biological mother, who now suffers from Alzheimer's. I felt depleted, drained, and alone, asking God "Why me?"

I remember at times I had no strength to move forward. I would lay curled up in the fetal position in my bed and just weep. At times, on my way to work, tears flooded my eyes to the point I could barely see. My family and friends rallied around me. My new life now consisted of still taking care of my family, but without the mechanic, as I neglected to take proper care of myself. I no longer wanted to do the things a woman would do for herself to keep herself looking and feeling like a lady.

MY W-2

Have you ever felt financially distressed from a year of tough encounters with bills and other weighty obligations? Have you felt anxious to call your human resource department to find out the exact date you would receive your W-2 forms in the mail? Have you ever been so desperate for a financial breakthrough that you painstakingly sought to borrow funds until you were able to file your taxes? After struggling and waiting for this financial burden to be lifted, there's such a sense of fresh air that grabs you. Similarly, this is what I experienced after running my laps in the waiting marathon.

The fate of God's hands had more in store for me than what I knew or realized. Unexpectedly, but, thankfully, God used my cousin to introduce me to a brother in Christ and friend of hers of over 15 years. Ironically, this soon to be love story happened on Thanksgiving Day. Furthermore, the irony continued with me discovering that this guy lost his mate as well. My cousin, Angie, thought it'd be a good idea for us to be "support buddies", although she was actually being "the matchmaker."

Prior to our Thanksgiving phone call, I ran into my cousin Angie at the nail salon. We hadn't seen each other in a while, so we were catching up with our lives. Since she had recently lost her mother and I had recently lost my husband. On the evening of Thanksgiving, Angie called me on speaker phone with her friend present. We all conversed. I was transparent about how that being my first Thanksgiving without my husband, I had cooked solo and in an effort to keep some kind of normalcy for my kids, I even tried cooking all of the dishes that my late husband usually made. We then talked about where we worked,which ironically, was for the same company. He worked there in the past and I was currently working there.

About two weeks later Angie, A.K.A. "The Matchmaker", had the nerve to invite both of us to her couples' Christmas party. "Are you kidding me?" This seemed a little odd to both of us — a couples' Christmas Party for a widow and widower. Considering we didn't know much about one another, it wasn't easy to get us to agree.

After several ping pong calls to myself and her friend, he suggested that I'd give him a call so that we could build rapport before meeting for the first time at this party. My first thought was, "I do not call men for dates." As you can see, God's hands were unfolding between us. So, I let my guard down a little. On Saturday, December 14, 2019, I decided to text Mr. K instead of calling because I figured people are generally busy on Saturdays. Since he did not respond to my text, I decided to call him that Monday night when I finished my work day. I don't know why, but, all day while I was working, the Spirit kept nudging me to call him. So, I did just that because it felt like I was calling someone I already knew. I was calm. I was at peace and I felt safe the moment Mr. K answered the phone.

Generally, I don't feel comfortable driving in rain storms, but while I was speaking with Mr. K, I felt safe and at peace because my tunnel vision directed me to our conversation more so than the driving conditions of the roads. I encountered detours on detours, but I never felt more free. Before I knew it I was home safely. We talked on the phone for the next four days; and, when we met in person, it was like we were long time acquaintances who were reuniting. The qualities that Mr. K possesses mirror the qualities of my father, which encouraged me to open up to him even more. My W-2 has now been delivered — a **widow** meets the perfect **widower**. I thank God for Mr. K, my King, a man who prays, helps with a pure spirit of generosity, meditates on God's word, and ministers to anyone at any time and any place:

characteristics of my father. Moreover, my W-2 thrives from helping strangers who are in need. He speaks the truth, in love, even if it may hurt one's feelings. He is not vindictive or intentionally harmful, but he exudes unconditional love. The wait is now over.

To Glory be to God! Life has its challenges. We don't have control over the things that happen; but, waiting on God is where all the control lies. We must operate in faith that He will answer our cries for help. Of course, sometimes we're eager to have what we want, when we want it; but, God, in His infinite wisdom, knows how to perform His will for our lives in perfect timing. His plan is perfect! He is literally always right on time.

Steps to Live By:

- We're given a choice to either live our lives according to the ways of the world or live it by God's word. God's plan will always prove the best results. Follow the plan of God. You will save yourself from trauma.
- Do the work! The word says, "Faith without works is dead." So, how can God do his work if you don't do yours?
- Delay doesn't mean denied. Despite how long you find yourself waiting, don't be discouraged in the process.

Kelly Page-Brown

7

Trust The Process

I come from a strict household. I was raised by both my mother and father. I am the youngest out of five siblings. My parents had me late in life; they both were in their mid 30's. So, I was the child who was extremely pampered — maybe even spoiled by them.

My parents began having children in their teenage years. My father worked at a chemical company, while my mother worked at a dry cleaners. Both parents played a significant role in raising me. I had the perfect balance. My father was a preacher, who taught me the power of prayer, how to be a respectful person, and the importance of having a relationship with God.

He always stressed, "Not every young girl develops into a lady." My father also taught me that a woman should carry herself with class and dignity. My mother, conversely, was more of a disciplinarian. She knew how to keep her children in line. She targeted having self worth and respect. My mother's dream for me was to go to college and have a successful career. She constantly said, "Respect yourself and your body or no one else will." and " Education is the key to success."

During my younger years, I obeyed my parents but life always has a way of teaching you valuable lessons. Often, when our parents lecture us about life, in the spirit of youthful cognition, which some deem as defiance, we tend to think, "You don't know what you're talking about!" I, too, toiled with those thoughts occasionally. However, one thing that I was certain of: I wanted to make my parents proud by becoming the woman they shaped me to be.

In our community, my parents were viewed by other people as noble adults, we, their offspring, were known to be respectful children.I grew up watching my father work diligently to ensure the well being of our family. I loved watching how my father would treat and interact with my mother. I knew that one day I wanted to become married and experience the same joy that my parents shared. Every young woman dreams of one day getting married. She imagines her father walking her down the aisle and being placed into the arms of her prince charming. Marriage became the ultimate goal for me.

The Compromise

Growing up my parents instilled life long values in me. Having a strong connection with God was non-negotiable. Finding my God-ordained soul mate and establishing a strong family of my own was another important goal. I was taught the importance of furthering my education and entering into marriage before having children of my own. My father believed that a woman should never lower her standards and have children before marriage—your body is God's temple. If a man is a part of your destiny, he should be able to wait for you and honor your standards.

Relationships don't always manifest the way you plan them. As women, we are sometimes involved in relationships that cause us to stray from our foundational values. As you become older, societal norms force you to develop anxiety about being married. Some women seem to think that if they're not married by a certain age, you're doing something wrong; they deem it taboo, allowing self esteem to seep in with overwhelming questions of "What's wrong with me?" or "Am I going to be single for the rest of my life?"

When these thoughts plague our mind, we tend to compromise our standards, settling for less that what we deem valuable, just to be married. Some meet men, without taking the time to get to know the whole person. The dating process becomes unnecessarily rushed, and before you know it, the woman starts to cohabitate with the man, hoping that's going to bring her closer to being married. She then find herself in a situation where she's cooking, cleaning, engaging in premarital sex. The perception is that these actions will bring the ring closer.

As anxious women, we find ourselves compromising our values and beliefs. Failing to stick to the plan that God has for us, we want to do things in our own way. We later develop the epiphany that we didn't get any closer to getting married, even after going through the rigmarole of lowering our standards. Then, we're prone to feeling used and unappreciated by that man.

When a man starts to date a woman, he has intuition that allows him to decipher if she's marriage material or not. Never compromise your values and beliefs, just to receive marital status from a man. If a man is truly for you, God will give you the proper signs. A man who's ordained for you will respect your values, pray with you, and always support your dreams and goals.

Society plays a major role in the factors mentioned above. Women tend to compromise after reaching a certain age to meet societal expectations. Media shapes our views as to what is the perfect age to be married. We also look at our friends getting married and wonder, "Why not me?" If you find yourself unmarried by "society's age of marriage", do not allow yourself to believe that God did you a disservice. According to Ecclesiastes 3:1, "For everything there is a season, and a time for every purpose under heaven." In other words, we have a particular season in life where things are destined to fall in line, according to the perfect will of God. God has not deprived you of anything! Trust what God has prepared for your life. Trust the Process !

Relationships

My first serious relationship was with a man named Leo. Leo was 2 years older than I was. He lived alone. I met Leo one day on my way home from work. He was charming, well dressed, and very polite. He knew all the right things to say to a woman. I was extremely impressed by his conversation. Leo and I exchanged numbers and soon started seeing each other exclusively. We began to spend much time together, laughing and enjoying one other's company. I learned that we both had a similar background—raised by both parents, religious, and goal orientated. The only conflict was that Leo didn't desire to have children. Initially, I felt as if the more he got to know me, he would possibly change his mind about having children.

This relationship began perfectly for me; he was my prince charming, or so I thought. I figured I had met someone who was like my father. He listened attentively to me and knew how to console me when I needed it. In my eyes, he was definitely married material.

Leo was a college graduate, who now worked for a computer company. So, I knew that he would be a good provider. When we went on dates, he would always open the car door for me. He would often ask me," What would you like to do today?" That was the first time dealing with a man when my thoughts and opinions actually mattered. Leo exposed me to various types of foods and restaurants in New York City. This kind of treatment made me become spoiled—like a true queen should be. On the weekends, Leo and I would go shopping. He kept me laced in all the latest fashions.

Leo and I dated for 2 years before my relationship took a turn for the worse. My car broke down, so I need another car to get back and forth from work and school. Leo offered to buy me a new car. I was ecstatic about him buying me a new car, a fully loaded Honda Accord. He made sure I had insurance and a full tank of gas every week. Although I lived on my own, I was never at my apartment. Every night, after work, I would go to Leo's house. He cooked dinner and prepared nice, hot, soothing, bubbly baths for me.

Unfortunately, things began to change after a couple of months. I started hanging out with my friends after work instead of going to Leo's. I would come outside from visiting my friends and notice that my car was gone. Leo would do devious things, such as having my car towed.

I realized that he thought his purchasing the car for me allotted him the opportunity to control my life. I would go past his apartment trying to find out why he had my car towed. He started conversing with me. Then, the next thing I knew he was slapping and shaking me.

My relationship went from being perfect to controlling and abusive. I was embarrassed to discuss what I was going through with anyone; but, eventually, I finally gathered enough courage to discuss it with my friends. Out of concern, they encouraged me to leave him and get things on my own. I knew I deserved better.

It took a little time for me to get myself together. I later found out that I was pregnant, carrying his child. I didn't know how to reveal the news to Leo. Somehow, I built up enough strength to call and ask him to meet me at a local restaurant.

I was entangled with many mixed feelings — extremely overwhelmed. I knew that I wasn't raised to have a child without being married, but I needed to tell him. I was hoping that he would be excited and change his mind about not wanting children. Leo did just the opposite. He aggressively shouted, " I told you I don't want a child, I love being a bachelor!" I couldn't believe what was coming out of his mouth. I felt used and humiliated. I later decided to have my child and continue with pursuing my Bachelor's degree. I learned to never let someone control me just because they're able to supply me with materialism. It's imperative to listen to what a man is telling you early in your relationship. Don't have selective hearing! *Selective hearing* is hearing what you want to hear, hoping that you can later change that person's mind.

A few years transpired and I had an urge to get back out in the dating world. I was a little nervous and hesitant because of the bad decisions I made in my prior relationship. Although I had my reservations, I decided to persevere.

My life began to change. I started working for an oil company. It wasn't my dream job, but it paid my rent and helped me provide for my daughter. I was a single parent. I had my degree, but found it difficult to obtain a job in my field. I literally went to work, came home, and took care of my daughter. Things were working out fine, but I was still lonely, longing for a male companion.

One day while at work, my local UPS driver came in to deliver a package. He randomly asked, " Are you single?" I responded by saying, " Yes." He replied, " I want to introduce you to my roommate." I was excited that whole day about meeting someone new. I felt like I was at a different place in my life: educated, independent, and more mature. The idea of marriage had come across my mind once again. I was tired of going to so many weddings, seeing others happy in their mates, so I started to dream again about getting married.

I was at work and a tall, good looking man walked into my job. He asked for permission from boss to speak with me. I walked to the door and he introduced himself to me. He said, "My name is Antonio, the UPS driver's roommate." We talked briefly and then exchanged numbers.

Antonio and I hit it off right away. He was a college graduate who was attending Law School. I started to feel like this could possibly be Mr. Right. Antonio worked at one of the most prestigious law firms in Livingston, N.J. So, his conversions were so intriguing. He educated me on various aspects of law, although my degree was in Psychology. We conversed for hours, discussing various topics, such as our political views.

Antonio and I spent much time together, but we weren't in an exclusive relationship. We both agreed that we would take our time to get to know one another before we committed to a relationship. He spent most of his time at my house. This was seemingly strange to me because every time I mentioned going to his house, he made up excuses. This was definitely a red flag for me. I had an inkling that something was not right. Unlike some women who ignore early red flags in relationships, I didn't.

Antonio was a man who also loved to travel. He would go to different islands with his coworkers during the year. I would often ask him to show me some of the pictures from the trip. He always replied with the line, "Someone else took the pictures." This instantly enticed my suspicion. He was too secretive — way too many closeted skeletons. However, I still pursued a relationship with him, but definitely with caution. A year went by and we were finally at a place of desiring an exclusive relationship.

Everything was going well until one evening when I called his house. The phone rang two times and then went to voicemail. I began to have a feeling in my stomach as if something was wrong. As women, we are born with a unique intuition. When a woman's intuition kicks, our body screams that something is wrong.

I put on my clothes and went over to his apartment. I rang the door-bell, but he didn't answer. I immediately became enraged and proceeded to sit in my car. As I sat in my car, I noticed a red car pull up. I got out of the car and approached him. He said, "That's my friend from work, she dropped me off." I didn't believe anything that was coming out of his mouth. I felt disrespected and humiliated. We stopped talking for a while but he still was calling me and sending flowers to my job. I ignored his calls and sent the flowers back to the florist. Eventually, I let my guard down. We started talking again and dating.

A couple of months had gone by and everything seemed to be normal. We both were thinking about taking our relationship to the next level. I was excited about planning our future together. I would finally be married and my daughter would have a dad.

My birthday has always been a special occasion to me. That year, Antonio arranged a special dinner date with all of our friends to celebrate at an exquisite seafood restaurant in City Island. I ordered my favorite seafood broil, while he ate chicken. Afterwards, the waiter brought out a cake and everyone began to sing "Happy Birthday" to me. Antonio pulled out a ring and asked me to marry him. I responded, "Yes." This was one of the best birthdays I ever had. I was finally getting married! I waited a couple of days later and asked him to set the date. He was very reluctant, for some reason, to settle on an actual date. So, I figured he needed more time.

Within a few months after this, I noticed a few changes in Antonio. He seemed to be hanging out a lot after work. I was starting to feel that women's intuition all over again. To my surprise, he was up to his old player tricks again. I received a phone call from one of my old high school friends, Ron. Ron said," Your boy is at the pub. Women are buying him drinks and sitting on his lap." Ron took pictures of him and sent it to my phone.

That night, I made up my mind that this was the end of my relationship. Later that same night, I also had a unique dream. God visited me in my sleep and warned me, " Leave that man alone. I didn't pick him. You picked him for yourself!" I woke up the next morning having an immense amount of clarity. I was so much in a rush to get married because of my age and societal norms that I failed to pray for my relationship.

The Turning Point

After my relationship ended, I began working on improving myself. I developed a better relationship with God. I worried less about marriage and consulted God in prayer on matters that I needed to work on internally. I realized what made me happy and started engaging in those things. I began to travel, read more, and focus on achieving my short and long term goals. I then understood that when the time was right God would present it to me clearly, as long as I kept Him as a priority in my life. I also made a promise to myself that I will never be in any more relationships that lowered my self esteem.

As time went on, I prayed for a new job and, thanks to God, He opened the door I prayed for. I was a kindergarten teacher working in Newark, NJ. This allowed me to meet Darrin, a tall, handsome, chocolate man that worked at the security booth.

Everyday, I would drive into my school's parking lot and notice Darrin checking me out. One day I was parking and looked out of my rear view mirror and he approached my car. I started to laugh because he looked a little nervous. I got out of the car and we both introduced ourselves to one another. The next day at work, Darrin handed me a CD to listen to. I took the CD and noticed that he had attached his number.

It took me two whole weeks to call him. I finally decided to actually call him. My conversation with him went really well! Darrin told me that he was a bachelor, who was previously married, divorced, and had raised two children. He was a seasoned man, a little older and was done with playing the immature games. This was definitely a plus because I was at a point in my life where I knew actually what I wanted. The best thing about my life at this point was I prayed before making any decision. If God didn't give me peace about making a particular decision, I decided to leave it alone. I was done compromising as I had assurance of my worth as a woman.

My conversations with Darrin went very well. I was most impressed with the fact that he had a strong relationship with God. He was a member of a church in Plainfield, NJ, which he attended regularly on Sundays. We spent endless nights talking on the phone and discussing the ministry and programs at our church.

My first date with Darrin was very different. I didn't allow him to come to my house, so he met me at a restaurant. We had a really great time, and at the end of the date, he walked me to my car. I expressed to him that I had a really nice time and I was looking forward to seeing him again.

He later called me on the phone to make sure I made it home safely. He suggested for our next date I could come over to his house and have dinner. I explained to him that I wasn't comfortable coming over to his house. He kindly replied," I understand!" I felt I needed to get to know him better before spending the night at his house. I have been there and done that! I knew that this time if I entered into a relationship, I needed to make changes. I couldn't keep doing the same things and expecting different results — that's insanity.

At that time, Darrin and I were involved in a relationship for 2 years. I stayed true to myself, my values, and my standards. Our relationship grew stronger as we drew closer to God, together. We prayed together and asked God to strengthen our bond. Darrin was always supportive of my academic endeavors. He also had a great relationship with my daughter.

Gradually, we both entertained the idea of getting married. I didn't get caught up in a ball of expectation because I had already been down this road in the past. I started to pray and ask God to give me a sign. God spoke to me and said, " Stay true to yourself and be patient." I actually received what God was saying to me.

Darrin knew that Christmas was my favorite time of the year. He and I were both excited about spending the Christmas holiday together. On Christmas night he asked me to come over to his house to unwrap my gift. On the way over there, I was so anxious to discover what the gift was.

I rang the bell and he opened the door with jazz music playing. I sat down on the couch and he got on one knee. He then pulled a ring out of his pocket and asked," Will you marry me?" Emphatically, without reservation, I responded, " Yes." I was so thrilled that I started crying — my emotions were high. Darrin then went over to his desk to pick up the calendar and set our wedding date. We got married in August 2012. Waiting for God and trusting yielded blessings. Being obedient made everything make sense. Trusting the process proved to bring forth great results. Waiting to get married changed my life tremendously. I discovered in the waiting process what made me happy. I had to revisit having a relationship with me. At the time that my husband came into my life I was already happy he just added to my happiness. I love everything about being married! I have a husband that is very supportive. He supports all of my goals and achievements. We both also have a spiritual relationship with God.

Ladies, I admonish you to Trust the Process......

Ladies, I hope that you enjoyed reading this chapter. Always stay true to who you are as a woman. Don't walk around thinking that you have the **secret sauce.** The secret sauce is thinking that what you have is different from another woman. Open up your ears and listen! What God has for you is for you ....

Steps to Follow

1. Have a relationship with God first.
2. Determine your relationship boundaries.
3. Respect yourself and command the respect from others.
4. Invest in your personal growth and goals.
5. Find happiness within yourself.
6. Be patient during the dating process.
7. Don't ignore red flags.
8. Don't have selective hearing.
9. Listen to what God is saying to you.

Kimberly Phelps

8

Crazy Enough to Kill

God doesn't care about me! I screamed this so-called truth inside of my mind. The words that kept slamming around in my head were hate, kill, hurt, liar, and cheater!

I was in a rage so profound that the only thought vibration throughout my body was to kill this man. I looked for objects around me to smash over his head when he finally came down the stairs from his apartment above the liquor store. I was really blinded by that much pain that the only thing I wanted to do was inflict an equal amount of pain on him. It was huge, jagged, and faded into a pale red with dirt and grime all over it. Yes! It was a brick staring at me begging me to pick it up so I did. I'm going to F' him up! I kept my finger on the doorbell ringing it incessantly, screaming at him from the street, to get his behind down here now! Theo was looking out the window, yelling at me to stop. Theo was the actual knife being jabbed repeatedly into my heart. How could one person cause this much rage in another?

It was around 9 pm and the hood was bustling. People walked by staring at me shaking their heads, but it didn't matter what anyone thought about me at this moment in time. I know you're living to see what happens next. Did he come downstairs? Did I smash his skull in with that dirty brick? Well, you just have to keep reading to find out, but for now I have to take you back to the beginning of this disastrous so-called love story: back before I had even met Theo.

The year was 1994, the year my son Kevin was born. I was 25 years old and a single mother of a beautiful, chunky, caramel colored little boy. It was definitely a rocky time for me. I knew nothing about babies. So, I turned to my mother everyday for help. It was a typical story: a young woman falling hard for a young man. I didn't know my worth and he didn't know his. I expected him to be a father to his son yet he couldn't even take care of himself. I realized the raising of our son was a forever task that I would have to take on alone, but that's another story.

My son was only 6 months old when the inevitable happened! Yes, you guessed it, I caught him cheating, sound familiar? I walked into his apartment. The door cracked open, and he was sitting on the couch lacing up his boots while a female was standing next to him. I knew in my gut they had been together sexually. Micah had a thirst for women. But, in retrospect, I realize most 24 year old men do. We argued. I yelled, cried, and screamed. She was backed into a corner as I directed my attention towards her- all of this happening in front of my son who was snug in his stroller unaware of the effects this day would cause in our lives forever.

"You want him! You can have him! I'm through!" Those were the last words I spoke to her for years until she called me and told me Micah had left her and their two kids for another woman. I was angry with him for being an a**hole again but they would eventually get back together only to cause me some of the worst pain in my life, but that's another story too.

So, back to 1994. I'm a 25 year old single mother of a beautiful boy living on Duncan Avenue in Jersey City in a three-story walk-up building that was fully renovated and very nice. I did well for my first apartment without a roommate. I had left the dorms at New Jersey City State College and moved in with two other friends in a nice three bedroom apartment in Jersey City, but not soon after I got pregnant and it wasn't what they signed up for. But, my roommate, Melissa, was a God-sent. She went with me to my lamaze classes and my doctor's appointments. However, I still felt abandoned by my Micah. When Kevin was born I left the apartment I shared with my roommates and moved on Duncan Ave. I was really on my own — no roommates, just my son and I. My mom helped me tremendously. I couldn't afford daycare and was making too much money as a preschool teacher to get financial assistance. My mom babysat him on the weekdays and dropped him off home every Friday evening. It was hard, because I didn't have a driver's license or car so we took the bus everywhere, me, Kevin and a stroller in the rain, the snow, at the grocery store, the doctor's office, everywhere. It was just me and him, luckily some of my co-workers at the Head Start center helped me get food stamps and WIC vouchers for formula. I had to forge some information but it was worth it for me so I could afford diapers, baby food and be able to pay my mom to watch him during the week. It would have been too much to handle without WIC and my mom.

Now, remember it was a great building where we lived on Duncan Avenue, but it was a three-story walk-up. I did most of my shopping when Kevin was with my mom, but when he was with me I had to navigate him, a stroller, a baby bag, and three flights of stairs. It wasn't an easy task, but we made it work. I did have a lot of freedom when Kevin wasn't with me during the week, probably too much freedom. I was considered to be very cute. I had naturally soft dark brown curly hair, chinkie eyes, and soft features. I had high cheekbones, a cute nose, and very shapely hips, booty and breasts. I was always considered "thick" because I loved food, however, I was constantly dieting with little success. I loved sweets, especially oatmeal raisin cookies! I'm sharing this with you, because I never had trouble attracting men. I had two or three boyfriends after Micah, but they never lasted long. It was a way to get over the loneliness to spend time with other men who found me attractive. Of course I was having sex. 26 years old by now—my own apartment and my son being gone most of the week did not lead to any good thing.

I ended up getting pregnant and having abortion number 3! The first one was 10 years earlier, my high school boyfriend. Number 2 was in college, I was 21. Old condoms are not a joke! I guess you're wondering why I didn't take the pill? Well remember, I've always been thick, I saw what those birth control pills and implants do to women my age, we blew up! So, there was no birth control for me, except condoms. Number 3 was on purpose, just not by me! The guy I was seeing at the time wanted to get me pregnant. He told me so when I told him I was having an abortion, and he'd already had 4 children by this time. By the time I met Micah, I was feeling the itch to be a mom, even though I wasn't married and didn't have any intentions to get married. So, when I discovered I was pregnant, this time I decided to keep the baby; and, you already know most of that story!

Let's fast forward to 1996, Kevin is 2 years old and a beautiful bundle of fat cuddles and kisses. I was striving to be a good mom. However,

I was young and didn't understand how my life directly affected him. I discovered that later in life. But, this is when I met HIM. The man from the beginning of my story. Yes, him, the one I was about to smash with a dirty brick.

It was a Saturday afternoon and I was struggling to get up the stairs with Kevin, bags, and a stroller. He was almost 2 years old by this time and he could walk up the stairs with my help but it was still a hard time. Suddenly someone lifted up my stroller and bags then carried them up the stairs. I didn't have time to say "No, I got this!", because I never liked asking people for help, but it happened so swiftly and suddenly that I was caught off guard. I scooped Kevin and carried him upstairs. I was happy and confused at the same time. Who is this man who helped me?

"I'm Theo, I live down the hall from you. Apt 8." He pointed to the door at the end of the hallway when we arrived on the third floor. "I watch you leave your apartment with your son. I'm not crazy or spying on you but I just wanted you to know that I see you. I just moved in last week with my baby daughter." I couldn't pay attention to his words fully. I was too busy focusing on his face. Observing everything about him. He was beautiful to me. The most beautiful man I had ever seen. No, really! He was a golden, cinnamon brown, kissed by the summer sun kind of man. He wore dark rimmed angular framed glasses, but behind them were deep, sad, soulful eyes under long, dark lashes. He was clean shaven and smooth skinned with thick but shapely eyebrows. He had a soft curly afro, perfectly faded on the sides with an afro pick stuck in the back. He wore a white fitted t-shirt that outlined the strength of his chest and muscular arms. His Levi jeans accentuated the definition of his thick thighs. I could see the ripples of his abs under the t-shirt moving rhythmically as he breathed. His scent filled my nostrils and made my head swoon. He smelled like Irish Spring and Downy fabric softener and when he smiled, his entire face lit up around beautiful white teeth. Yes, he was gorgeous and I was entranced. He took my breath away and I knew at that moment he would be more than my neighbor at the end of the hall.

"I'm Kim", I said, smiling as if an angel was facing me. "O.K, I'll be around," he said, as he walked down the hallway. His swag was sexy, cool, and masculine. Yes, he had swag, oh so much swag! His walk was slow, captivating, and deliberate. He kept his shoulders erect and his head held high. I gasped slightly and went inside my apartment as he opened the door to his. I didn't want him to catch me watching him, but it was too late, I smiled at him and went inside. This was a feeling I never had in my life! I was 27 years old. Nothing this profound had ever happened to me with a man. I didn't understand the feelings I had for a stranger. My body vibrated. I was having a heightened experience that was confusing and exhilarating at the same time. I couldn't stop thinking about him, smelling him, feeling his presence around me. What was this?

I didn't see him again until 3 days later when I heard a knock on my door. It was a Tuesday and I didn't have Kevin. He was with my mom. I peered through the peephole and saw HIM standing there! He wore a white t-shirt again that stretched over his muscular frame and blue jeans. I thought to myself 'he knows how to show off that body without overdoing it, but the same outfit again? That's strange.' I opened the door, excited to see him, but I had to play it cool. I mean really, Kim! You only met him once! "Hey, what's up? Theo right?" I thought I appeared to be calm.

"Yes, Theo. I wanted to know if you had pepper? I'm making stew and ran out." He had a sparkle in his eyes as if he knew that I was privy to the fact that it was only an excuse for him to come and see me. "Sure do," I said, smiling uncontrollably. "Come on in." He was in my apartment. We were alone together. My heart was racing, as my body screamed for him. I have to be honest if this is my story. It is these very human and natural emotions that cause us a lot of pain and damage if we don't learn to control them, instead of them controlling us. I had never been taught about emotions this strong before. It was like I had lost self control and all the feelings inside had hijacked my brain. I wanted him sexually! But, it was different from any of my past relationships, even with Micah. Considering the men in my past, I always liked them; I thought they were attractive, however, I had NEVER felt like this before. What is that when you meet someone for the first time and you immediately want them in a sexual way?

So, now we're in my small kitchen and I'm fumbling through the cabinet looking for pepper. I could feel his body heat next to me. Was it mutual? O.K, he found me attractive, but, like I mentioned before, I had never had a problem attracting men. Did he feel this crazy thing that I felt? I finally found the pepper and handed it to him, wondering what he would say now to stick around. "Thank you Kim. Do you like beef stew?" "Yes!" I thought to myself, "He's asking me questions. He's not ready to leave."

"Umm, yes. Love beef stew. Why? You're gonna give me some?" I stood in front of him, wearing a short black flirty, girly summer dress. I loved the summer, so I felt breezy, light, and beautiful around him like a cool summer breeze flowing into the open window in the kitchen. I breathed his scent of Irish Spring and Downy as the breeze brushed against my skin. I was feeling lightheaded again, so I leaned against the wall in the kitchen, smiling at him.

"Yes. I wanted to invite you and your son over for dinner. Where is he, sleep?"

"No, he's with his grandmother." The smile was pasted on my face. Those words I had just spoken meant something totally different than the obvious.

"Would you like to come over for beef stew? It'll be finished in about an hour. Come by then. I'll leave the door open." And those words definitely meant more than dinner, in my mind.

"O.K. I'll see you then. Will your baby girl be there?" I know I was blushing!

"Kenyatta? No, she's with my mom." His eyes twinkled again as he opened the door and moved in that sexy, rhythmic swag down the hall. Even his walk had me warm. What is happening to me? What is about to happen to me in an hour?

The hour went by quickly! I had to shower, paint my toes, shave in all the right places, brush my teeth, find something cute and casual to wear, and of course smell really good, like he did. I had this fabulous orange scented body mist from the Body Shop. When it melted into my skin it released this pungent, enticing aroma that I knew would intoxicate him. I walked down the hall, 65 minutes later, not to seem too anxious and knocked on the door, then slowly and quietly let myself in. It smelled wonderful in his studio apartment. I breathed in the scent of beef stew and I immediately felt comfortable. As I looked around I noticed that he only had a kitchen, a bedroom, and a bathroom, no living room. I felt a frenzy of emotions exploding inside. I had never wanted someone like this before. That desire, the smell of the stew, being alone with him, and the scent of my orange body mist and his Irish Spring drove me crazy.

He was standing in front of the stove stirring the pot of stew when I walked behind him. "Wow! Smells delicious." I said moving closer to him and the pot of stew. My body was close to his now, I peeked over his shoulder, my chin resting on him, he dropped the spoon in the pot, turned around and wrapped my arms around his waist drawing me in tight. He hugged me with this grip that was strong, forceful, and oddly sensual. My face was buried in his chest and I breathed in his scent squeezing my arms even tighter around him. I didn't dare to look up into his face because the thought of kissing him frightened me. All of this was too intense for me. I pushed away gently and sat down at the kitchen table. "I'm starving. Do you have dessert too?"

We enjoyed delicious food together that evening. We discussed being single parents. His daughter was a little younger than Kevin. I could see her little shoes lined up in the hallway. I finally asked him about her mother. "We'll talk about our exes another day if that's ok? I want to learn more about you." Even the sound of his voice did something to my soul. It was similar to his walk, slow and deliberate but grammatically correct. He didn't use slang or broken English. He carried himself like a real man, a very serious man, though. That's the one thing that made me uneasy. How did he interact with his daughter if he was this serious all the time? How would he interact with Kevin? But, I stored those questions in the back of mind because the sexual attraction was greater than any concerns I had.

We talked for hours about everything but our exes. It was like the big pink elephant in the room that we ignored. 'Where is this girl's mother? She's not even 2 years old. What woman leaves their daughter at 2 years of age?' These thoughts couldn't be stored away. It was at the forefront of my consciousness but I wanted to respect him so I didn't mention it. It's not everyday that you see a 27 year old single father raising a baby girl.

I didn't want to leave but he had to go pick up his daughter from his mother's house. We hugged good night, and I prayed he didn't try to kiss me. I know I would've jumped his bones if that had gone down. No kiss, thank God! "Everything was delicious Theo, but next time I need dessert please. Oatmeal raisin cookies," I said, my arms still around his waist, looking up into that absolutely gorgeous face. Focusing on his lips that he licked gently before he spoke.

"Anything for you Kim. I was hoping we can do this again next Tuesday?" He didn't smile at me, but he stared at me, looking down deeply into my eyes, pulling me closer to him, wrapping me inside of his arms. It was incredible that I didn't explode right there.

"Sounds good to me. Will I get to meet your daughter Tuesday?" I asked, hoping he'd say "No". That's messed up right? But I wanted us to be alone. I wanted to get to know him better, without the distraction of his baby girl.

No really, I did. He was fascinating. He was from Jersey City, born and raised. He had grown up on Palisades Ave, went to Catholic schools, and was just honorably discharged from the Marines after doing 10 years. I was still waiting for the answer as he pondered the question. "Let me see what I can do. Maybe, my mom can pick her up from daycare on Tuesday and she can spend the night there. I'll let you know."

I could feel all of him (I know, too much information but it's my story and it's the most natural thing in the world! The erection of a man! So, enjoy the details!) as our bodies were held tightly together. He gave me a soft peck on the lips, then another, then another, and oh boy!!! We were full on kissing. (I know you want to hear more about this kiss. I'll tell you soon, but for now, let your imagination run....)

It was finally Tuesday and for some odd reason I really wanted to meet his daughter after all. I was curious about her and wanted to see their interaction. How was he as a father? This was important to me because I imagined us as a couple, and I needed someone who would be a good father to Kevin. There was a knock on the door. I looked through the peephole to see Theo and a beautiful cocoa chocolate baby girl standing next to him holding his hand. She had thick eyebrows just like her father, big almond shaped eyes, and wore her hair in 4 thick long black braids. I opened the door and greeted her right away. "Hi, this must be Kenyatta." I tried to be as upbeat and pleasant as possible as I wanted her to like me. Not just because she was Theo's daughter, but because I genuinely love children; and, this little girl was absolutely precious.

"Say hi Kenyatta, this is Ms. Kim. Remember I told you we were coming to visit her today?" He spoke to her as if he was speaking to me. She was less than 2 years old and not an ounce of baby- talk escaped from his mouth.

"Hi Ms. Kim" she said softly, but didn't return the bright smile I gave to her. She was very cautious of this new woman in her father's life. Even at 2 years old she seemed wise beyond her years. She looked around my apartment then spotted some of Kevin's toys. "Daddy can I play with this?"

I shook my head yes, but he pointed to me and said, "You have to ask Ms. Kim if you can play with her son's toy."

"Ms. Kim, can I play with this toy?" She didn't smile or seem excited over the toy, but she was interested in playing with it. She was very much like her father. A serious little girl with an old soul. I was amazed at how well she spoke for such a young child. Kevin was just the opposite. At 2 years old, he hadn't even formed a complete sentence yet.

"Kenyatta, I have a son about your age, Kevin, but he's not here right now, he's with his grandmother." I was sitting on the couch now so I could be closer to her level.

"I go to my grandma's house too." She said this as she continued to play with the toy.

"Are you ready to come over to my place for dinner now?" Theo asked me, with a little smile on his face.

"What's so funny?" My eyes scanned his body, appreciating how handsome and masculine he was.

"I enjoy feeding you. I can tell you like to eat and like to cook for you." Well that was a joy to hear. A man who likes to cook for ME! I had always thought that my weight was an issue for men, even those who found me attractive. In my mind I was always thinking that they probably wished I was slimmer. But with Theo I never felt that way. The way he looked at me was enough. I could see in his eyes he thought I was sexy, desirable, and beautiful. I know what you're thinking...did they do it yet? Well, NO! Not yet. He had to pick up his daughter — no time for that. But, a woman can just tell when a man finds her desirable, it's energy I guess. Energy can't lie.

I spent a lovely evening with Theo and his daughter, observing them together. He was very matter-of-fact with her. Treating her like she was a little adult. When she walked into the apartment she immediately removed her shoes and lined them up in the hallway next to his. She then walked into the bathroom, stood on a small step and washed her hands, scrubbing her fingers with a small nail brush. She walked into the kitchen and sat at the table waiting for dinner. After dinner she went into the bathroom with her nightgown, brushed her teeth, and said 'Daddy I'm ready for my bath now." Theo fixed a nice warm bath for her and we sat in the bathroom together as she played with the toys in the bathtub. I would catch glimpses of that sadness in his eyes as he watched his daughter playing in the tub. I would snap him out of it by asking him about his family and Kenyatta's school. He was very open to talk about almost anything except her mother. But, for me, it was always present, now that I was imagining us as a family. The perfect blended family, right? You already know the outcome of this love story, but I'm giving you the insight to truly understand why I wanted to kill this man. Just keep reading. Boy, does it get juicy!

Although I met Kenyatta, I didn't want Theo to meet Kevin until I saw how he interacted with his own child. I can see he loved her but he seemed uncomfortable with being affectionate, playful, and engaging as a dad. It was about teaching her, instructing her, establishing routines and organization. I figured that it was attributed to 10 years of being in the Marines. Theo was in Desert Storm and witnessed some things that most of us had never experienced, but it seemed like the broken relationship with Kenyatta's mother is what caused him to be disconnected from his daughter; and, crazy as it was, he reminded me of MY father. Now this was very weird. I never had a good relationship with my father. He was never warm, loving, or affectionate. He never once told me that he loved me or was proud of me. It was always instruction, discipline, rules, chastisement, and negative programming.

So, let's get into my father now. I know you want to hear about the hot and steamy love making sessions between Theo and I , but this is not a "dirty novel." It's a story about me, a woman who finally discovers who she is by encountering pain, challenges, and struggles while waiting for the promises of God to show up in her life! How can I really write about my journey without digging into my childhood? So, here we go! Strap on those seat belts and take a complicated ride into my youth.

II

I was doubled over with pain, rocking back and forth, going from sink to toilet over and over again. It was that time of the month but it was also the weekend I would have to visit Shaka, my father. "Mommy, I can't go visit Shaka. I have cramps!" I was yelling and pleading with my mother to have pity on me. 'Please don't send me there', I would say in my mind over and over again. "Mommy, call him and tell him I'm sick, please!" I knew my mother felt sorry for me. She left Shaka when

I was just a baby. He was a very, very, very difficult man to live with or get along with. My mother told me that one day Shaka came home and demanded my mother give over her entire paycheck to him! Now I don't know about the black women in your life, but the ones in MY life would NEVER do that!

My mother told him exactly that. So, he told her to get out if she doesn't do it. "I'll get out, don't worry about that. But, I'll leave when I'm ready." My mother saved for two months, I was about one year old at the time, she packed us up and walked out. My father balled his eyes out crying for my mother to come back, she never did! Do not mess with a black woman's money!

So I grew up in a dysfunctional home. I didn't realize it was dysfunctional until I went to college and studied sociology. My mother was a single mom of three children by three different men. We didn't see a problem with that growing up. We each had our own dads. My older brother, Terry, had Carlton. Carlton was married to my mom, her 2nd husband. Carlton was fine! If you want to imagine Carlton, think about those real slick and handsome Motown crooners that made the young girls fall out on the floor, that was Carlton. I mean that was my brother's father, but, truthfully, I was crushing! I mean I was only 8 or 9 years old at the time but I knew a good looking, well dressed, nice smelling man with money in his pocket at an early age.

Then there was my younger sister Tisha. Her father was Chuck. Chuck was illiterate. "Had to spell his name with an X", my mother would say to me. He was a janitor at a local Catholic school, who came up north from Tuskegee Alabama to make a living for himself in the 50's. That marriage only lasted a few years. He was abusive to my mother. Thank God she made the decision to kick him out! In the middle of that was me. Yes, the middle child. My father was Shaka a.k.a Wayne. He had legally changed his name years earlier to *Shaka Zulu Ramses*! I guess you can tell, he was very much into African History. My middle name is Nefertari, an Egyptian queen. My father was brought up in Chicago. His family owned several chicken farms in different parts of Chicago, selling their chickens, eggs, and other products to the well-to do black Chicagoans of that time. My grandparents were affluent entrepreneurs in Chicago during the 1930's. My father came from money, but a tragic turn of events would change his life forever, thereby affecting my life as well.

When Shaka was 8 years old he was playing with firecrackers with his father. The family told the father that it was too dangerous for little Wayne to play with firecrackers. His father disagreed and let him continue on with the fun. My father didn't release the firecracker in time and it exploded in his hands. Now, at 8 years old in the 1930's this affluent family had a "deformed" son that they were ashamed of. His father was burdened with extreme guilt that he destroyed himself with alcohol. Shaka's mother had a mental breakdown after the accident, and , seeing her husband devastatingly destroy himself with liquor, they committed her to an insane asylum where she deteriorated into a shell of her once beautiful self. A woman of deep ebony complexion, graceful and proud. One of Chicago's high class beauties. My father would go visit her at times and cry because she didn't recognize her own son. The Phelps family disowned and shunned my father because of his deformed hand. He would spend most of his youth and adolescence on the streets of Chicago eating out of garbage cans and sleeping in alleyways. Sometimes he was put in foster homes but experienced cruelty and abuse so he would run away and make a life for himself on the streets.

It wasn't until he was about 15 years old when life finally took a better turn for Shaka. He was taken in by a foster mother, who was good to him. He told me that Ms. Mattie Mae was the closest thing he had to a mother after his own mother was no longer able to take care of him or herself. I'm writing this through the words Shaka shared with me as a young woman. Ms. Mattie Mae loved my father as her own son. She fed him good, hot, nutritious meals. She washed his clothes, gave him a warm bed to sleep in, made sure he finished high school, and he became a star football player his senior year. She changed his life, because, as a complete stranger, she showed him love even when his own family wouldn't. When he was in his early twenties he heard about the Great Harlem NYC! It was his destiny to be a part of the New York City Renaissance movement and it was in NYC that he met the esteemed and honorable Marcus Garvey! Shaka became a Garveyite and Black Nationalist. He would be steeped in by black pride, but the pain and damage of racism, prejudice, and abuse from his family, black foster parents, and Jim Crow would shape his life and in turn shape me as a girl and later in my womanhood.

It was this man who raised me. He raised me with a level of pain so deep that it was nearly impossible for him to receive love, or give love in the manner that was needed by those around him, including my mother and I. It was from that space of mental, emotional, and physical abuse that I was reared. So, all that hurt, pain, fear, anguish, abandonment, low self-esteem, trauma, guilt, and shame was now projected onto me. I grew up dreading every other weekend, becoming physiologically ill whenever I had to see him, crying and begging my mother not to send me. But, the courts ordered it and I had to go. I was subject to a father who never hugged me, asked how I was doing, he praised me for anything, except graduating from college. He condemned me for every fault and many things about me disappointed him. I was never right: never accepted for just being me. I never felt appreciated or valued by him. He tried to teach me how to hate others, because of his hate. He berated me for my belief in God, as I started to find my own path. He only believed in his intellect, he had once told me. I feared my father. I respected him out of fear, not love. He was a 6 foot 4 big strapping hulk of a man. He intimated people by his sheer size, especially me.

His trauma became a part of me. I internalized his feelings of in-adequacy because he projected them onto me. Those negative states of mind caused me to have extremely low self-esteem from early child-hood. I was bullied in school because I didn't like or love myself. I felt that no one liked me, how could they when I didn't like myself? I didn't have many friends in school and the ones I did have left me for people who had a better love and respect for themselves. I repelled people because I never thought I was worthy enough to be liked, definitely not worthy enough to be loved.

But, even as a child, I knew that something was not right with Shaka. He had never abused me physically; he just didn't have the capacity to show love, which wasn't his fault. He only outpictured what was inside of him. But, my intuition as a child told me that Shaka was not my "REAL" or biological father. This is something I would tell my mother each time I had to go see him. "Mommy, why are you making me go see him? He's not even my real father!" I would cry uncontrollably. The anguish of spending hours with him or an entire weekend with him killed my spirit daily. I was in a constant state of fear and anxiety. I suffered with stuttering and had to go to remedial classes in school due to my trauma. No one understood this at the time. I didn't comprehend the negative effects my relationship with Shaka had on me growing up and how I carried it into adulthood.

I had a strong intuition that he was not my real father, but my mother would deny this allegation for more than 20 years, insisting that Shaka was my biological father. When I turned 18, I told my mother that I was never going to see him again. I was not going to be tortured by the incessant criticism and domineering spirit of fear that he had over me. I was fighting for my life and peace. I turned to food and television to help me deal with the trauma of my youth. They became my friends, my escape from my life. Where others may have turned to drugs, alcohol, or sex to cope with trauma, I turned to food and television. It caused me to be self-isolated and extremely shy, passive, and introverted.

When I finally had a boyfriend in high school, I allowed him to exploit me sexually because I was so happy to be out the house and around someone who gave me attention. I experienced my first pregnancy and subsequent abortion. It wasn't until I decided to do the necessary therapeutic work, that I began the self-healing process. The first step in that process was when I turned 21. It was when my mother finally told me the truth.

III

So, now you want to know what this big truth is, like you can't figure it out. I know you're smarter than that. But, we'll get back to that later. It's time to get back to the steamy stuff. I'm sure everyone reading my story may have their own story of imperfection, lust, greed, envy, jealousy, gluttony, hate, vengeance, shame, guilt, fornication, etc. This is my raw version. If I can't be transparent and real within my own story for fear of judgment then I have no business being a writer, period.

Love, sex, lust, desire — it's real life stuff. We've all had to deal with one or more of those emotions. It doesn't matter if you're a Believer or not. We are human and that is how we've been designed. It is up to us to execute self-control, but that doesn't negate the fact that it's real. As a 27 year old non-Believer, I wasn't trying to control myself. I wanted this man and he wanted me. We had a connection that I couldn't comprehend; but, I needed to explore it. It had to take its course.

So, Theo and I finally had a chance to be alone in the middle of the week. Him and Kenyatta had come over one weekend to meet Kevin. The children meshed very well. Most children at that age do. They aren't bogged down with prejudgemental thoughts that isolate them from the world or their own self-hate that keeps them locked away and afraid to make real connections. These are toddlers who can feel one another's energy and play together authentically. I observed how Theo interacted with Kevin: the same way he did with his own daughter. I didn't see the joy, the enthusiasm, the lightheartedness that most people feel around toddlers. He was stoic even around my son. There wasn't any play wrestling, swinging him around, playing horsey, or playing alongside him with his toys. But, because my desire for Theo was so strong, I ignored that and focused on what I wanted, not what my son needed.

Now we're alone, at his apartment. We had just come in from a beautiful night of strolling by the riverfront in Manhattan and having dinner at a low-key, dimly lit restaurant in the city. It was a romantic date and I was feeling warm, sexy, and tingly all over. I knew this was the night, finally. When we got back to his place we had some wine, soft jazz, and candlelight. The smell of my orange body mist spray filled the atmosphere, but we were both sticky from the summer night and decided to refresh in the shower, together!. OMG!!! Wait! You're not ready for this. You can't handle this. I could barely handle it myself. I was like wow! Oh my! Am I dreaming?

I stood there, wrapped in a large black towel, gazing at this beautiful black man. His skin was cinnamon golden brown, smooth and soft to the touch. His body was lean, muscular, and exuded sensuality. His thighs were strong and well defined. He removed the towel and helped me into the warm shower. He stepped in and began to lather the wash cloth with Irish Spring soap. He turned me around and began to wash my neck and back gently. Then, he moved gingerly down my body, caressing me softly as I felt the warm lather flow around my skin. He turned me around to face him. His eyes were drinking in all of me. Washing me with the washcloth, scrubbing my stomach, hips, and thighs, moving gently over my breast, and the secret areas of my body.

I had never taken a shower with a man before. I was 27 years old and a man had never washed me, caressed me, or touched me like that before. I couldn't understand why this was happening to me. Why was I experiencing this level of intimacy, sensuality, sexuality, and desire? But, I was melting in it. I was inhaling it all, from his beautiful body, the feel of his touch, the sweet smell of his breath, the tenderness of his touch, the warmth of the soapy water, and the fresh scent of Irish Spring soap. So, this is what I had been missing?

In all of my other relationships, I engaged in standard missionary style. It was routine. It was nothing like this. It was only about them, not caring about pleasing me, but I didn't know any better. I didn't know what I was doing as a teenager and a young woman in my twenties. It was missionary style, they enjoyed it, and I was good. I had never had a sexual orgasm. I'd heard about it, I'd read about it, I even watched it happening in pornos. (No, I wasn't always saved.) I had never experienced one. But, I knew this man was different. I knew he was concerned with satisfying me sexually. I took a clean washcloth from the towel rack to wash him next, but he took it away from me and started to wash himself, watching me, staring me in my eyes, as he moved the washcloth along the beautiful lines of his body. We both rinsed off. He dried me off. Then, dried himself. He lifted me and wrapped my big legs around his strong back. I was amazed at how easily he lifted me, as if I had the weight of a child. He carried me to the bedroom. I did NOTHING that night. He did EVERYTHING! He made me feel like I was the most desirable woman in the world, more desirable than the hottest movie star or singer. I felt like he wanted to bask in everything relating to me.

We laid in one another's arms all night, falling in and out of sleep, waking up in the middle of the night, and doing it all over again. We drank wine and listened to soft jazz as the candles flickered in the background, while the cool nighttime summer breeze blew through the windows. It was like a dream. It was me awakening to a sensuality I never knew existed. I was becoming a woman who was releasing something that had been stored up inside for years, my own sensuality, my own need for a heightened sexual experience, and how it felt to be pampered and catered to in this way. See, Theo was my first. The first man I ever truly loved. The first man who gave me an orgasm. The first man who asked for nothing in return. The first man to have me in so many directions, that missionary style never came up. He was the one that opened my flower and set my petals on fire. He exposed the wild side of me, the adventurous side of me, the creative side of me. I never understood the power of beautiful sexuality and intimacy until he opened me up to it all. I became a different woman with him. During that time, I didn't claim to be religious, but I always knew there was a God. I understood, then, that God made men and woman as sexual, powerful creations, both equally having the receptors to experience sexual bliss. I knew that sex was not a shameful act, but a powerful exhibition of love and intimacy when you engage in it with the right one. He was that one for me. I was falling in love. My heart, mind, and soul was open to him.

Theo and I became an official couple after that first night. I met his family and he met mine. We spent evenings together during the week with Kenyatta, and with Kevin on the weekend, when my mother would bring him home. I worked through the summer months at Head Start. So, It was just the three of us until Friday, when Kevin came home. Theo was getting closer to Kevin; they had a good rapport. Kevin would snuggle up under Theo's arm, while he played with his favorite toy. Kenyatta would snuggle in my lap, as I read her favorite book. Sometimes we would hangout at his place and other days it would be my place right down the hall.

Sometimes my mom would keep Kevin for the entire weekend because she planned special outings with him. Theo would get his mother to watch Kenyatta and we would have the weekend to ourselves. We went to concerts, jazz boat rides, dinners, and house parties with his friends. We would come home and make love for hours and hours. I was happy as the months rolled into the holiday season. He would pick me up from my mother's and come up to hang out with the family. We went to concerts with his mom and stepdad. Kevin and Kenyatta were like brother and sister. It was this season of my life that shaped me the most as a woman and a mother. I realized that I could love someone else's child just as much as I loved mine. Kenyatta was a part of me too now. We were together almost everyday. She needed a mother, Kevin needed a father, and Theo and I needed each other.

But, this wouldn't be a story worth telling if the antagonist never reared their ugly (but beautiful) head!

IV

I knew something wasn't right when Theo came over that day. He was usually very sensual and touchy with me, but this day he came in and sat down on the couch with a very serious look on his face. "What's going on? Why are you so upset?" I grabbed his hand and sat on the coffee table across from him.

"Kim, I'm sorry, but I still love my wife." I pretended not to hear him. I had to pretend not to hear that, because if I had accepted those words immediately, I probably wouldn't be here right now writing this part of my story. The part of my story that shaped me as well. The part that tore the spleen out of my body, gutted my intestines, and stomped mercilessly over my heart! Yes, THAT PART!

Over the past 10 months of our relationship, we finally opened up about our exes. I explained to him that I had loved Micah and wanted to start a family with him, but I caught him in an act of infidelity with his ex-girlfriend. Micah was an absent father. So, I was grateful to have Theo in our lives. He told me about Kenyatta's mother, Adrianna. They had been separated for over a year when I met Theo. They were still married, but legally separated. She moved to California with her oldest child she had before she met Theo.

He further shared with me that they met while he was stationed in California. They dated for a year before they drove to Las Vegas and became married. Their marriage was rocky from the start. Neither one of them was ready to be faithful. They cheated with other people where they were stationed and the rumors got out. It took a serious toll on their marriage. Theo was relocated to another station and they were finally able to mend their relationship; so, they decided to stay together. This is when Adrianna became pregnant with Kenyatta. Not long after she had Kenyatta, their relationship started to go downhill again. She wasn't taking care of the baby, she started cheating again, and, consequently, he started cheating as well. Both of them tried to drown their pain in alcohol and that only contributed to the breakdown of their marriage.

He decided to leave the Marines with an honorable discharge. He left California and moved back to New Jersey, where he had the support of his family. He asked her to come with him, but she refused. So, he left with his daughter and filed papers for a legal separation. He was back home for a year, living with his family, until he found the apartment on Duncan Ave, which is where he met Kevin and I. He explained to me that his relationship with her mother was very volatile and that he never wanted to be that way with me; and, to be honest, he never was. There was a level of mutual respect that we had for one another that never lent itself to any type of physical altercation.

However, at that very moment, I was in front of him, pretending that I didn't hear the words that would turn my life upside down and smash it on its head! He uttered those dreadful words again, and, this time I squeezed his hand tight, hoping he was going to say: "But I love you more." To my surprise, those words never came.

"Kim, I'm sorry. The last thing I wanted to do was to hurt you. I love you Kim, but that's my wife and I want to be with her. I want to make it work with Kenyatta's mother."

I stared at him — speechless. I couldn't even compute what he was saying. This was MY man. This was the man who I fell in love with. This was the man who made me feel incredible. This was the man who was becoming an amazing father figure to my son. This was the man who allowed our families to grow together. This was the father of Kenyatta, the little girl who I grew to love as my own. Now he was sitting on my couch telling me he still loves his wife and wants to be with her. I finally caught enough wind to ask a question before I would start to break down.

"She's back, isn't she?" I knew the answer before I asked the question. My entire body felt ill, as if the stress of a million people were piled on top of it. I could feel my stomach drop and the ball in my throat swell up, trying to hold back the flood of tears that was about to break forth.

"Yes Kim. She's here now, down the hall with Kenyatta." He watched me, prepared to move suddenly, not quite sure what to do next. Kim I'm sorry, don't hate me please. He stood up from the couch and walked towards the door. I'll try not to put her in your face Kim. I won't do that to you." He walked out the door as I sat there. He walked away from me and everything we had created together within the last 10 months. He walked away from my son, he left us. I felt raw and rotten inside. I felt useless and vulnerable. I felt unworthy, unloved, and uncovered. The tears came accompanied by a wrenching sob that filled the space in my apartment. I doubled over with gut wrenching pain rocking back and forth on the couch as if I was about to literally die of a broken heart. I laid there on the couch for 3 days, calling out from work. In retrospect, I'm glad that this took place during the week, so that Kevin was not home to witness me in such a condition. For three days I didn't eat, drink, or bathe. It was pure pain. I had never experienced this kind of pain before.

I finally gathered enough strength to go to work, physically, but I wasn't fully present, mentally or emotionally. I had checked out. I would go into the bathroom to cry, wipe my face, and then try to play with the children. During the following month, I had lost 20 pounds and walked around in a state of depression.

I saw the two of them leave the building at the same time as me, twice. I noted the specific times and made sure I left earlier, so I wouldn't have to see them. It was as if a knife was stuck in my back each time I saw them leaving out together. I tortured myself, picturing him making love to her. I couldn't play with my son. I had lost all joy for living. I would lock myself in the bathroom and sob for hours. Kevin would knock on the door yelling, "Mommy crying! Get Theo Mommy!" Kevin was three years old by now and he had grown close to Theo. He was able to speak in short sentences now. Those sentences would echo in my soul for years afterward. We were a family, but Theo and Kenyatta were no longer around. "Mommy let's go see Theo and Kenyatta," he would say to me, after eating dinner in the evenings. The tears would flow even harder, knowing how much this was affecting Kevin, it just continued to break my soul down everyday.

Then, one day there was a knock on the door — Kevin was with my mother at the time. I looked out the peephole and I saw her, Andrianna! I recognized her immediately. Why was she here? I never bothered them; I left out earlier or later then they did. I didn't call him, I didn't knock on the door, I left them in peace. But now she had the nerve to knock on my door. I opened the door slightly and said "Yes!"

"I'm Adrianna, Theo's wife. He told me that he gave you a key to his apartment. Please, bring it to me when you get a chance. Thank you." She walked away back down the hall. I knew she wanted to speak to me; she was curious about me and I was curious about her. What did this woman have over him that he would leave me to go back to her?

I found the key and walked down to his apartment; the door was left unlocked. I went inside and she sat at the kitchen table waiting for me. "Hello Kim," she said, "You can sit down." I sat across from her looking at her to find the beauty he saw in her. She was a very beautiful woman. I could see Kenyatta when I looked at her. She appeared tall, even though she was sitting. She had a cocoa brown complexion like Kenyatta with a stylish short haircut. Her skin was smooth and she wore minimal makeup. Her nails were short but polished and she sat there, examining me as well. "So you're the woman who stole my husband's heart?" She asked this question rhetorically, but I answered, "No", anyway.

"He's walking around here depressed, not talking to me, not eating, not playing with his daughter. He tells me he loves you and he's hurting because he had left you alone to save his family." I was shocked to hear this coming from her. She didn't have to tell me this. She could've just taken the key and left me alone. "I think he wants to come back to you. But I'm letting you know now, that's MY husband and he'll never break up his family for you. I can smell you all in his apartment. We've washed the sheets and we can still smell that orange scent. I just want you to know that I'm back for good. Do you have a baby with him?" I was startled by this question. I'm sure she asked him that but I guess she didn't believe him. I later found out that she conceived another child with someone else during their separation and she had left that child to come back to Theo and Kenyatta. I told her no, pushed the key closer to her, and walked out.

I left his apartment still feeling betrayed by him, but, at the same time, owning a strange sense of power considering the words she said. Why did she tell me how he was feeling and that he still loved me? That didn't benefit her at all. The next day, Theo was at my door asking to see me. I let him in, eager to hear what he had to say. "My wife spoke to you yesterday? Look, I told her that I still love you. Kim I'm confused. I want it to work out with my family, but I'm also still in love with you."

He grabbed me by the waist and buried his head in my neck. I started to massage his scalp with my fingers, feeling the soft curly texture of his hair, smelling his scent, feeling his breath on my neck and his body close to mine. That's all it took for us — all we needed to be back in bed together. We made love on the couch and then he got up and walked out and went back down the hall. I felt used and ashamed, but slightly prideful that he still wanted me and even shared this information with Andrianna. We would go back and forth like this for weeks. We were sharing him and trying to win him; he had become a prize and the woman he loved the most would win. The lease was up on both of our apartments and I knew I had to move out. I asked Theo to move in with me; he was torn. If he moved in with me, that would signify that I won the prize. He would leave his wife.

Theo did move in with me. We found a nice place on Old Bergen Rd. in Jersey City. He did it. He left his wife and the mother of his child for me; but, predictably, this only worked out for a few months. The guilt attached to being with me and Kevin, instead of his daughter, didn't allow him to rest comfortably. He left 4 months later.

Anger took over me. While I understood that his heart was with his family, especially his daughter, and he had always yearned for his daughter to have her mother in her life, it was extremely devastating to me.

Ultimately, Kenyatta had her mother back, but her father was living with another woman and her son. His family was still broken. He had come from a broken family as well. His father had walked out on his mother when he was 14 years old. He never wanted to repeat that cycle; it tore him apart, but he had to leave me, he had to keep his family together. So, he left. How could he continue to do that to his daughter, being raised in a broken home? He had to put her first, so I understood that.

So, OK! If I was able to understand why he left me, why did I attempt to smash his head in with a brick? Oh, wait for it, it's coming!

V

The pain of losing Theo taunted me for years. I raised Kevin alone in our apartment on Old Bergen Rd. I remembered where Theo had put his grandmother's chair in the corner of the living room. I replayed in my mind the way we made love in the back bedroom, how he would sleep for hours after working the night shift as a mechanic, and the days we spent in one another's arms on the sofa. When suffered from a cold, I served him hot tea and ran a warm bath for him. I remembered the way he touched me, how he would cater to my every need intimately. It was beautiful in the beginning, all three of us living together, but we could all feel the emptiness without Kenyatta. It was another pink elephant lurking about, waiting for us to acknowledge her.

When he finally left me, I wasn't surprised. I predicted it. I actually respected him more for leaving than if he had stayed. Strange, right? But, it's true. The separation from Theo impacted my life more than anything else: more than Shaka, more than the multiple abortions, and more than Micah cheating on me. His absence from my life shaped me. I questioned myself all the time. I felt empty and unwanted. I didn't like who I was, I was a mess. I was a single mother raising a son whose father was barely around.

I was left in a state of depression for years; and, that's when I met Akeem, my youngest son's father. I met Akeem when I was at my lowest point. I had no self-confidence, no self-love. I was depressed and lonely. The worst state of mind to be in when meeting someone knew. Why is that you ask? Well I didn't realize it then because I hadn't done the inner work so this is in retrospect. You attract people with the same negative energy that you exude: people who take advantage of your pain or people who are in a similar state of hurt and pain. Like attracts like!

I met Akeem through a co-worker. He had just been released from doing 5 years in prison. He never disclosed to me what his crime was, but I knew it was drug related. He was living in a halfway house in Jersey City. He landed a decent job and was making his way back into the world again. He was also a Sunni Muslim, a religious affiliation he had converted to while in prison. We were two hurt people, who found one another only to hurt one another even more. We became a couple because we were both lonely, hurting, and insecure. I had converted to Islam hoping to find myself and to find the missing piece of happiness that seemed to elude me. We planned to get married Islamically before being intimate. There was no sexual attraction between us at all; but, we were clinging to one another for some sense of normalcy or hope. He explained to me that we didn't need to be in love to get married — that we would grow to love each other.

I had to convert to Islam first. So, I took my shahada and became a Muslim. I went to the Mosque and sat in on the meetings with the sisters. I practiced my prayers and different ways to wash and contort my body during prayer. I practiced fasting during Ramadan and knelt to pray 4 times a day. I read the Quran and listened to Islamic teachings. I wanted God or Allah to save me, to rescue me from myself, from this inner pain, but nothing happened. Akeem moved in with Kevin and I. He was distant with both of us. He went to work, came home, ate dinner, read the Quran, and went to bed. Since he was devout in his beliefs, I could no longer have a Christmas tree or listen to secular music, not even Christian holiday songs. I had never practiced any religion prior to meeting him, Christianity and Islam. This practicing religious stuff was all foreign to me and I felt stifled and imprisoned mentally with all the rules I had to learn as a Muslim woman.

I wore the hijab, the long garments, and the head covering. I covered my hair and avoided exposing my skin. I hoped this would bring me closer to God; so, my soul could heal, but it never did. I didn't convert for me. I actually converted because I was lonely and desired to be wanted by someone. Akeem didn't love me. He just wanted to be a different version of himself, taking on the role of a ready-made father was a great thing in Islam. But, there was no love. The day before the wedding, I told him that I couldn't go through with it, I didn't love him, and we were making a mistake. I was finding my voice again, I knew what was going to come of this marriage. I was already in escape mode! I was trying to break free from the disaster before it hit hard. But, he wouldn't hear of it.

"You can't call off the wedding. My mom already paid for everything and the invitations already went out. My mother would be devastated." He was very upset. Not disappointing his mother was more important than disrupting our whole lives by living a lie. But, instead of standing up for myself, I gave in to the pressure. The next day we were married at a Chinese buffet banquet hall somewhere in NJ. Our entire families were there, excited to see us tie the knot in this Islamic wedding. We both wore Islamic attire: he wore a cream colored Muslim suit and I wore a creamed colored Muslim dress, custom made. After the ceremony by the Imam, we ate and proceeded to our first dance. It was a dance of complete and utter regret, it was a dance that ushered in months of trauma and hurt. It was a dance I knew I never should have had. As we were dancing, my thoughts were, "This is the worst mistake of my life."

Akeem was cold, withdrawn, and distant. He had no joy inside of him — no fun, no life. The week after our wedding, we had a cruise to Puerto Rico that his mother gifted us. The day of the cruise, he decided he didn't want to go. He laid on the couch brooding, shutting down, and not talking to me about how he was feeling. I called his mother. She spoke to him and convinced him to take the trip. This was our honeymoon. It was the honeymoon from hell! We argued. Then, we gave each other the silent treatment. He stayed in the cabin, while I ventured out alone. We barely ate dinner together because we weren't speaking. We were never intimate. There was no kissing, holding hands, or sex — nothing! On our wedding night, I tried to be sexy for him. It was supposed to be our first sexual experience together, but he was repulsed by me. "I'm not sexual attracted to you. I can't do this with you," he said to me, with no emotion in his voice.

This was my life for almost a year. I was in a new religion that I didn't understand, a new marriage with a man who was repulsed by me, and I hated myself for being so weak and timid that I let all of this happen to myself. I ate to fill the void and loneliness. I ate, watched TV, went to work, offered prayer, and cooked for him and Kevin. That was my everyday routine. That was my life and it was slowly killing me. I gained 30 pounds after the wedding, gorging on cookies, cakes, candy, and Halal Chinese food. For New Year's Eve, he slept, while I sat in my son's room watching the ball drop eating Ring Dings and Hostess cupcakes alone. It was at that moment that I knew I had to free myself. A few weeks later I got up the nerve to ask for a divorce! He tried to talk me out of it but I was set. "You'll learn to love me!" He kept repeating those words over and over again. But, I didn't back down this time. I was fighting for my life!

I had a doctor's appointment the day before our appointment with the iman for the divorce: my yearly check up. Yes! You guessed it! I was pregnant! I WAS PREGNANT! Now, some people don't believe me when I say this, but to this day, I still don't know how that happened. Akeem and I was never intimate, we never had sex, that I can remember. I'm thinking he had his way with me while I was asleep. Don't judge me! Crazier things have happened. Now, I'm not saying this was an immaculate conception, but I am saying I can't recall when the impregnation took place. Nevertheless, I was devastated! How can this be happening to me? I'm about to divorce this man and now I'm pregnant?

Abortion number 4 was the first thing I thought of; but, I promised God that I wouldn't have anymore abortions. I might seem matter-of-factly about it, but those abortions took a toll on my psyche. I often thought about what my three children would've looked like. What personalities would they have had? However, if I kept this baby I would be tied to Akeem forever! I had to be free of him! I had to be free of Islam! I was screaming inside! I was about to have a nervous break-down and there was nothing I could do about it. How do I stop a train from crashing? I was that train and it was head on lightening speed! "God help me please!"

The next day, I met Akeem at the iman's office in Newark. He asked us a few questions and then pronounced us "Divorced." We received a formal document in the mail weeks later. I didn't tell him about the pregnancy. I still didn't know what to do. Do I honor my promise to God by having the baby and have to deal with Akeem forever or do I have abortion number 4 and be free of him forever? I called my mom and grandmother, who were both living in Florida. "Mommy, I'm pregnant. I don't know what to do." I was 29 years old. It was only one year ago that Theo walked out on me. Now, here I am in another messy situation.

"Kim, keep the baby, we'll help you. You're not alone." My mom and grandmother were both on the phone, trying to calm me down and trying to stop the tears. I decided to keep the baby, because I knew my mom and grandmother had my back. I knew I could get through anything with my mom on my side. She was the strongest woman I knew and my grandmother was the wisest. I finally told Akeem I was pregnant and he was happy. He wanted me to keep the baby.

"We have to get remarried. We can't bring a child into the world out of wedlock, Allah doesn't allow it." Akeem said this with hope in his voice, thinking this would convince me to remarry him. Nothing would have convinced me of that. Nothing! I was confused at why he wanted to remarry me anyway. What was wrong with him? I knew he wasn't happy with me, but it seemed like happiness wasn't important to him. He was willing to be in a loveless marriage for the sake of the baby. Me? No way! I was never going back.

During the pregnancy, Akeem came to the apartment to read to the baby and talk to the baby inside of my womb. It brought me anxiety, discomfort, and stress. I didn't want him around me. I had divorced him and now he was here every other day so he could speak to the baby and read the Quran to the baby. I couldn't take it anymore. It had to stop. He had to go. This caused a dissension between the families. They thought the baby wasn't his because I didn't want Akeem around me. They questioned it constantly and caused arguments between the families. My mom had moved in with me to help take care of the new baby when it arrived. She was the buffer between me, Akeem, and his family. The stress of it was taking a toll on me, and, later through my work, I would discover it took a toll on my unborn child as well. The stress a mother goes through during pregnancy directly affects the health of the child, mentally, physically, and emotionally; but, that's another story.

I finally gave birth to a beautiful, milk chocolate, silky-haired baby boy. He looked like a black Indian. I named him Kamal. He was a blessing. Kamal was bright eyed and full of energy. He looked, smiled, and laughed. He was plump and affectionate. His whole family gathered around him and he was loved. Akeem, however, didn't bond with Kamal, because he didn't think the baby was his. He asked for a DNA test, and, when Kamal was a few months old, we got one. It was proof that Akeem was the father. I thought he would step up and be active in Kamal's life, but he didn't. He said he would give up legal rights to the baby. He didn't want the responsibility of being a father. Well, that wasn't happening. My son needed a father. I took Akeem to court for child support, but he had quit his job; so, I got no child support from him for nearly 5 years. He was at risk of losing his driver's license. That was the only reason he contacted me — to pay me my back child support, which his mother paid. I took him off the system and he paid me $200 a month for the following 13 years until Kamal turned 18. However, he was rarely in his life: an absentee father, again. I prayed for a father for my son.

So, it was Kevin, Kamal, and I. We were a family — and, my mom, of course. My mom kept Kamal during the week and I picked him up on Fridays. By that time, I had a license and a car. My mom moved to East Orange, NJ. She was there for me again, showing support. I don't know what I would've done throughout the years if it wasn't for my mother — God rest her soul. She passed away from cancer in 2008, 9 years after Kamal was born. But, during that time, she loved and cared for her grandchildren. She would fly or drive down to Florida with the boys to see my grandmother, their great-grandmother every year. It was difficult for them both when she passed away.

So, I was a 31 years old single mother with two sons. I questioned everything about my life. How did I end up here? Why did I lack the happy loving relationship that white women on TV had? That's all I saw growing up. These happy-go-lucky, nuclear white families with two parents, a big clean house and well-fed, well-educated children living in a middle class home. Why did I have to be the 31 year old black woman, single mother, raising two boys in the hood with fathers who barely came around? Why did I have to be a statistical stereotype? It was those questions that eventually led me to the greatest discovery of my life, but, before that happened, I had to deal with the past that was still a haunting part of my present reality. Yes, you guessed it: Theo.

You still want to know why I wanted to kill him at the beginning of this story, right? And where does he fit in now? Well I'm about to tell you. This is where it really gets crazy!

VI

Kamal was only a year old when Theo reached out to me. It had been two years since he walked out on me. I had too much going on, raising two children alone and dealing with my own inadequacies, low self-esteem, 30 extra pounds of baby weight, and not earning enough to take care of two children alone, to worry about Theo. So, I was surprised when he called me. He had a new baby girl and I had a new baby boy. His wife became pregnant not long after he went back to her; but, the kicker was that she had left him and both the girls AGAIN! Yes! He walked out on all three of them and went back to California. Now, I know how it feels to be a mother and a woman who has to raise her children without the presence of a father, but I'm not a man; so, I could only partially relate to his pain.

She left him and Kenyatta when she was just a newborn, leaving Theo to navigate fatherhood alone, but when she returned from California, asking him to take her back and let her be a mother to Kenyatta. He agreed, because he wanted and needed to keep his family together. He left Kevin and I to be with his family. But, he was alone again, raising two little girls by himself. At that time, I wasn't in touch with his pain; I saw it as a chance for us to be together again. I thought it was God orchestrating the whole thing. I knew that we were supposed to be family since the moment I met him. It was as if the world was correcting itself, lining things up the way I knew it should be.

He invited us over so we could all meet again. He had a new apartment over a liquor store on the "Hill" in Jersey City. It was a large, bright apartment with two bedrooms. The girls shared a room and Theo had his own room. They met Kevin and Kamal for the first time; and, we met Kenyatta again and the new baby girl Zoe. I just knew we were supposed to be a blended family. They needed a mother and my boys needed a father. I never stopped loving Theo and I believed he felt the same way. It was exciting and beautiful to think about our future together — all of us sharing a life, growing up together, facing the world together, maneuvering through the challenges of life together. His estranged wife would no longer be a factor. She walked out on him again. He could never take her back. It was a clear path for me to slide back in where we left off. This was destiny!

Theo, myself, and our children started to become a family. We ate dinner together a few nights a week, went to the park, helped with homework, cooked meals together, and really enjoyed one another's company. When the children were with their grandparents, Theo and I would go out to jazz clubs in the City, movies, dinner, and house parties. We were parents, but we were still young, in our early thirties. We needed to have fun, to be sociable. I was back in the mix now — meeting more of his friends, getting reacquainted with his old friends, and hanging out with his mom and step dad again. He would take me to pick up the boys and we would sit around talking to my mom for a few hours before we left. We picked up where we left off two years prior. You see, Theo was my first real love, the kind of real love that Mary J. Blige sings about. It was that first kind of love that you watch in a major motion picture. It was the kind of the love where you call sex, making love; and, that's what we did best — make love.

I was extremely self conscious about the extra 30 pounds of baby weight, the expanded stretch marks, and the stomach pouch: the warrior marks of childbirth! But, Theo didn't care about any of that. He kissed each stretch mark, licked my body as if it was creamy chocolate ice cream, caressed and massaged my baby pouch with oil, and devoured my body with a tenacity that made me feel more beautiful than anything in this world. You couldn't tell me I wasn't sexy and desirable, even with all this extra me! That's how Theo always made me feel and nothing changed. The way he loved me, the way he held me, touched me, and enveloped me with his love was beyond beautiful. It was the air I breathed. It was my joy in the evenings, my piece of heaven in the mornings. It was how we expressed our love for one another and it bonded us, I thought forever. But, I soon realized nothing is forever, not when it comes to relationships, definitely, not my relationship with Theo.

It was just us in his apartment this evening. The children were with their grandparents. We had just finished making very sensual love when he told me about this nightmare he had a few nights earlier. "I was asleep when I felt this movement under the sheets. I was paralyzed as I watched it slither across my body under the white sheet. It was a python snake twice the length of my body. It started to wrap around me and slowly tighten its grip on me. I couldn't breathe. I was gasping for air, trying to call out to you. You were in the bed next to me, but I couldn't move. I couldn't make a sound. I was suffocating while you slept right next to me." I listened deeply, staring at his face as he relieved this nightmare. He has always been afraid of snakes ever since he was little. It was his worst fears coming to pass in his dreams. Only to him, it didn't feel like a dream until he woke up and gasped for air in a panic attack.

We didn't understand the meaning behind the dream, but he said something very significant after that. "Kim, I don't know if it's God or the devil that brought us together." WOW! What!? Who says that to a young woman in love with her man? Maybe the devil brought us together? Then, he continued and what he said after that changed my life forever! "I know you don't go to church and that you had converted to Islam; but, you were never truly connected. I know you're searching for a higher meaning to life. I don't know much, Kim, but what I do know is that Jesus is one with God the Father and that Jesus is the light, the way, and the path to what you're searching for. I grew up in church all my life, my grandfather is a pastor, and I know beyond a doubt that Jesus will save and heal you. Jesus is the answer you're seeking."

He told me this while we laid in his bed, both of bodies soaked in sweat, candles flickering in the room. I watched his face, looked into his eyes as he spoke those words to me. I could feel his sincerity. He had experienced the presence of God many times in his life, so he spoke with authority and conviction. He had been stabbed and shot multiple times in his young life, but he knew God protected him from his own foolishness. I laid there listening, not saying a word, confused and surprised that he would tell me this after making love to me. He reached into his side drawer and pulled out a large box and placed it on the bed. He opened the box and pulled out a large, beautiful, leather bound Bible! Yes! A Bible!

I had never owned a Bible. I didn't grow up in church. My first church experience was at 16 when I visited a friend's church. I went a few times, but never returned. Now this man who I was crazy about gave me a Bible. He opened it up and wrote my name inside, "This Bible is given to Kimberly Phelps, From Theo Stevens, Year: 2000." I took the Bible and flipped through the pages. I had appreciated its beauty, but at the time I didn't understand its significance, nor its power; but I loved the gesture. My man gave me something that was important to him as it was something he thought I needed. In my mind, however, I didn't need a Bible, I needed him. What can a Bible do for me? Theo, on the other hand, had given me life again. He was the only thing I needed. The problem with that, is he wasn't mine like I assumed. I was the side chick. YES! ME! Now how did I find out? I'm about to tell you.

It was an average day with the children. They had just finished eating and were playing games together. Kamal had just learned to walk so he was everywhere, trying to get into everything. I was chasing him around the apartment when Theo's doorbell rang. He looked out the window, said he'd be right back, and ran downstairs. I looked out the window and saw him talking to a woman. It was an older woman, at least 10 or 15 years older than us. Theo was only a year older than me: 32. I wondered what he was doing messing around with someone that old? I figured it was an ex girlfriend, someone he was seeing after his wife had left. I didn't think much of it, I was back now and any other woman in his life would have to bounce. I was his soulmate.

The Universe orchestrated this relationship, no doubt. So, when he came back upstairs, he told me she was just a coworker and would drop by sometimes just to check up on him and the girls. So I didn't press. I was there, in his apartment with his children, in his bed. Whoever she used to be to him, she is that no longer! Kim is BACK! Or, so I thought.

It was MY turn to be the one standing outside. I came by his apartment, and usually he would ring me in right away, but this day was different. This was the day that shaped me, formed me, and broke me, more than any day before and more than any day since. Now, at 53, I'm writing this story.

"Hey, let me up. I have groceries." But he didn't let me up. I kept ringing the doorbell until he finally came downstairs. I knew the second he refused to let me in, my life as I knew it was over — that all the pain from the past would come rushing back like a force wind ready to destroy everything in its path.

"Kim, I can't let you up. My friend Dawn is upstairs.", he said so nonchalantly, with no emotions or apologies.

"You mean your coworker Dawn? The one who comes to check on you and the girls? You're not letting me upstairs because SHE'S there! What the f — k is going on?!!!" I was screaming! "Tell her to leave Theo, tell her to leave, now!"

"I'm telling her about us. I'm breaking up with her Kim."

"You're breaking up with her, NOW? Wait a minute, you've been seeing her all this time? Wait, she's your lady Theo? That's your girlfriend? You mean I'm the side chick? You've been cheating on Dawn with ME?" I felt enraged, disgusted, and insane. Yes! Insane! The anger was boiling red hot inside of me. It was as if my brain couldn't compute what was happening but my body could.

I saw that brick. That faded red brick that told me to pick it up and smash it at his car window. I lifted up my fist and swung at the side of his head! Bam! He saw me about to swing again and caught my arm before I connected. I swung at his face with the other fist and whacked him across the cheek. He had both my arms, restraining me, so I went to bite his nose, but he twisted his face and backed away. Then, he swiftly turned me around and put both arms in a vice grip. I couldn't free myself. I was screaming and crying. The groceries were all over the ground. It was late, around 9 pm. The city was still bustling and the neighborhood people just watched and kept walking.

"Kim calm down. I'm going to tell her to leave. She's leaving tonight I promise. I'll call you when she's gone. Stop being like this. This isn't you Kim. I'll handle it." He kept saying this to me until I finally calmed down, on the outside, but inside I was an atomic bomb ready to detonate. He let my arms go, backed away slowly, and went upstairs. I could see her in the window watching the whole scene. It was her turn to look down at me, the way I looked down at her a few nights before. So I waited and waited — and I waited. I sat in my car that was parked outside of his apartment, waiting for her to walk down the stairs.

I waited for hours, upon hours, upon hours, until the sun was coming up. I sat in my car for nearly 8 hours, crying, shaking, cursing, heaving, talking to myself, yelling at God, hating life, hating Theo, hating Akeem, hating Micah, hating my father, hating myself, hating my mother for lying to me, and hating this Dawn woman — hating and hurting, an agony so deep that I felt as if my brain was cracking. I could feel myself slipping, becoming someone else, a person I didn't know. I heard the voice in my head say, "kill his a.." It was a small voice, but it kept talking to me. I kept listening. "Kill him now," the voice kept insisting, waiting for me to take action. But, how would I do it? Ring his bell until he came downstairs and hit him over the head with the brick?" But what if he called the police on me for ringing his bell at 5 am? The police? "But, I'm a teacher! I have two sons that need me. NOOOOO! I can't kill him."

So, I looked up at his apartment one last time, still hoping to see her leave at 5 am, but that didn't happen. I imagined him making love to her and I felt sick inside. I was sharing him again, but this time it wasn't his wife. I was able to understand him leaving me to keep his family together, but he left me again for HER — this old Dawn woman. He did it to me again: used me, stepped on my heart, crushed my entire belief in real love. He made it into a joke, made ME into a joke. He destroyed my soul to the core, to its depth. Why was I even alive? Why the hell did God bring me here? What the hell is wrong with me? Why do people treat me as if I'm nothing? Why doesn't anyone love me? Who am I God and why do I even exist? Do I exist just for all this pain in my life? I drove myself home only a few miles from Theo's apartment.

I put on my nightgown and grabbed the Bible that Theo had given me days before. I crawled into my oldest son's bottom bunk bed, bible tucked into my arms, and I cried uncontrollable tears of anguish. As I laid there I cried out to God and said, "If this Jesus of the Bible is real then you better come and save me NOW because I'm losing it! If you're real, Jesus, then help me NOW! I cried myself to sleep; but, during that restless night, I had my first encounter with the Spirit of Jesus the Christ!

It was a dream and I knew that because I woke up; but, it was as real as the hands on my wrists. This dream was as real as the labor pain from giving birth. This dream was as real as an ambulance siren screaming in your ears.

Here it is: the dream that transformed my life forever! I was in the ocean, with turbulent wild waves surrounding me. I was swallowing water, drowning, fighting for my life. My arms were flailing in all directions. My legs thrashed about me. The night was cold and pitch black as I started to sink into the tumultuous waters of the deep; but, suddenly, in the distance, I saw a figure cast out a life saver tied to a long rope. I grabbed hold of the life saver, wrapping my arms around it and gripping it for dear life, literally. I could see the figure pulling in the rope. Pulling it steadily until I reached the shore. I crawled onto the sand, catching my breath, and looked up to see the figure standing over me. There was no face, just an outline of a figure; but, I knew it was Jesus the Christ! I knew Jesus had saved me. It was morning when I woke up. I was different. I was very different. I felt like a new person. A person who was injected with a strength I had never known. That day, I got dressed, walked to Theo's job, and asked to speak to him outside.

I looked him square in the eyes, unflinching, unwavering, with a determination and audacity I had never had in my life before. "Don't ever call me again Theo! Don't ever reach out to me or try to contact me ever again. I'm through with you." I was calm and deliberate. "You're serious." He said almost in shock.

I walked away from Theo that day and never looked back. I was never tempted to go back. It was never even a thought that crossed my mind. I knew God had changed me. Jesus did a new thing inside of me that I wasn't able to do on my own. My life from that point on was to learn all I could about God and His son, Jesus Christ. I am who I am today because of that experience. I've had my struggle with belief over the years, questioning God when I've discovered my own revelations about spiritual things. But, what I'll never waiver on is my belief that God loves all people, and God's love is the greatest spirit ever to exist, and we are the conduits and the instruments of God's powerful love! Love is a Spirit! We must accept that God loves us before we can start to heal from past traumas; but, we must be willing to come to God in spirit and in truth. That means spirit speaks to spirit, and the truth is you are, we are spirits, gods, created in the image and likeness of our creator. We are God's thoughts expressed into this natural realm from the spiritual realm.

You were created for a purpose and you are more than enough; actually, you are incredible, beautifully, and wonderfully made — God's masterpiece! Now go out and serve God's love to the world! In retrospect, I learned much from my relationship with Theo — actually more than you may realize. Our story doesn't end there. It took 25 years later for Theo and I to talk about the relationship that shaped me and formed me the most. That's another story! Just wait!

Key Life Lessons

- Accept God's unconditional love. Learn who you are and why you are loved so deeply by the Source.
- Never allow a man to define the value that you were fashioned with from the Almighty Father. Instead, be persistent enough to wrestle with yourself to discover the fullness of your value and allow it to compliment his.
- Prioritize your mental and emotional well-being. If you are broken, you are of little worth to your ordained mate.

References

1. Neuroscience News, W. C. (2018, November 5). Happy childhood memories linked to better health in later life. Neuroscience News. Retrieved July 29, 2022, from..................... https://neurosciencenews.com/childhood-memory-health-10145/#:~:text=People%20who%20have%20fond%20memories ,by%20the%20America%20Psychological%20Association

2. American Psychological Association. (2010). Childhood memories of father have lasting impact on men's ability to handle stress. American Psychological Association. Retrieved July 29, 2022, from https://www.apa.org/news/press/releases/2010/08/childhoodmemories

3. Female: Maurene. Maurene - Name Meaning, What does Maurene mean? (n.d.). Retrieved July 29, 2022, from http://www.thinkbabynames.com/meaning/0/Maurene

4. Coughlin, S. (2017, August 15). Today celebrates the mysterious end of the virgin mary's life. The Assumption Of Virgin Mary 2018 Spiritual Meaning. Retrieved July 29, 2022, from https://www.refinery29.com/en-us/2017/08/168108/the-assumption-of-mary-spiritual-meaning